Democratic Socialism

Somewhere Between

Democracy and Tyranny

William R. Joseph

Table of Contents

Introduction: 7

Chapter 1: The Evolution of Socialism   11

Chapter 2: The Appeal of Democratic Socialism   32

Chapter 3: How Capitalism is Perceived by Socialists   39

Chapter 4: Democratic Socialism–Not About Freedom   50

Chapter 5: Social Conditioning   59

Chapter 6: How Socialism Leads to Tyranny   66

Chapter 7: Capitalism in the United States   76

Chapter 8: Personal and Fiscal Responsibility   82

Chapter 9: Identity Politics and Victimhood   92

Chapter 10: Cultural Differences   102

Chapter 11: Between Democracy and Tyranny   112

References: 119

Democratic Socialism

Somewhere Between Democracy and Tyranny

ISBN: 9798662868076

Printed by KDP Amazon, Inc, in the United States of America

First printing 2020

Introduction

At about the end of World War I, the more affluent in society were regarded as upper class or aristocracy, nobles, etc.   Most were landowners and those who were economically, socially, and politically upwardly mobile. The general citizenry were common people who went about their daily lives of running community-oriented businesses, eateries, retail stores, etcetera, and providing various trade services.   By socialist standards, most citizens would be considered poor, debt-ridden agrarians whose lives were ruled by the policies and taxes established by the political class of the day.   At least until the masses said, "enough is enough."

At these times, an often self-proclaimed champion of the people would arise and gain popularity among the common people by promising to topple the aristocracy, level the playing field, and bring equality and prosperity to all. Think Bernie Sanders, Ocasio-Cortez, Nancy Pelosi, and rest of the Squad. Historically, these self-appointed champions have curried favor with the populous and assumed representative leadership roles in government through exploitation of the public's general ignorance and lack of political experience.   Without fail, some of the first and largest planks in their political platform are broadly and vaguely defined infrastructure and community building programs and social relief programs.

Equally predictable is the assertion that every new program will allegedly to be paid for by taxes on the wealthy. Notable examples throughout history of self-proclaimed champions of the people include Mussolini, Mao Zedong, Stalin, Hitler, Franco, Ceausescu, Idi Amin, Saddam Hussein, and Gadhafi. Everyone of those named came to power through some variation of the promise of equality and prosperity for all at the expense of the current ruling class. It is a matter of historical record that, once elected by the people, they kept their new found power through repression, terrorism, and punishment of anyone who was perceived as a threat.

This socio-political cycle is not a recent phenomenon. Seven centuries before Christ walked the face of the earth, Aristotle reportedly taught that oppression was the time-honored policy of ambitious, self-seeking men. And that tyrants limit citizens' freedom of association, discourage education of every kind, and frown on social clubs in the belief that discussion groups and common meals engender self-respect and self-confidence among the people. Similarly, Xenophon taught that the tyrant fears the brave lest they plot, and the just lest the people prefer to be ruled by them instead. Recent and current events in the United States suggest this philosophy still holds true.

Generally, tyrants employ bureaucratic spies and various forms of the media to disseminate and implement social conditioning of the masses. Re-education of free thinkers and prosperous entrepreneurs is typically accomplished through exorbitant taxation, burdensome regulations, social unrest, and civil war. This approach has the effect of keeping the general public distracted, mutually distrustful, and politically powerless. On the bright side, tyrannies usually only last about one generation even when they masquerade as pseudo-constitutional governments. In Greek history, tyrannies were often succeeded by democracies. In recent world history, not so much.

Philosophically, the concept of representative democracy is based on self-government of the people, by the people being governed, and for the mutual benefit of all the people. The fundamental value of life in a democratic republic is the guarantee and protection of fundamental human rights, liberty, and freedom. Core tenets of government by the people are equal justice, promotion based on personal and professional merit, personal freedom, respect for the law of the land, civic engagement, and free enterprise. In free societies, citizens are free to own property, pursue education and vocation of their choice, engage in political discourse where friends are made by conferring rather than by receiving personal favors. The more experienced are sought out for wise counsel and guidance. The wealthy are assumed and expected to know something about managing the world of finance. Representatives of the people are selected on the basis of relevant life experience and a proven track record of knowledge of the science of government.

A common failing of representative democracy is that it can easily devolve into a direct or absolute democracy. In an absolute democracy, sometimes too much power is wielded by too many people with too few controls. In 1859, John Stuart Mill wrote the book *On Liberty*, where he used term "tyranny of the masses" to describe this tendency. Narrowminded demagogues soon appear, driven by passion and the intoxication of public admiration and power, to influence public opinion.

These often incompetent and unscrupulous officials get elected by an uninformed and uneducated populace through flattery, feigned compassion, and fear mongering, much like we see in the U.S. federal, state, and city governments today. The end result is generally the same. The citizenry is preoccupied with business and family life and so trust others to tend to the affairs of government, assuming protections under the sovereignty of law. Eventually however, the needs of municipal growth and commerce, and personal political interests supersede the needs of the individual.

Those in positions of power seek to stay in power by creating centralized government and promoting a Robinhood narrative of "nothing in excess for anyone, and equality for everyone," typically at the expense of the middle class. Throughout history, this narrative is frequently characterized as Democratic Socialism. Let us look at how it started and where we are likely headed.

Chapter 1

The Evolution of Socialism

If socialism has a future, it may well lie in some form of market socialism. Market socialism promises neither the utopia of the early socialists nor the brave new Generally speaking, socialism is a social and economic doctrine that calls for public rather than private ownership or control of property, both real and personal, as well as natural resources.

From the socialist perspective, individuals do not live or work in isolation but live in cooperation with one another. Therefore, everything that people produce is in some sense a social product, and everyone who contributes to the production of a good is entitled to a share in it. Society as a whole, therefore, should own or at least control property for the benefit of all its members.

This conviction puts socialism in opposition to capitalism, which is based on private ownership of both real and personal property as well as the means of production and allows for individual choices in a free market to determine how goods and services are distributed.

Socialists complain that capitalism necessarily leads to unfair and exploitative concentrations of wealth and power in the hands of the relative few who emerge victorious from free-market competition. These people then use their wealth and power to reinforce their dominance in society. Because such people are rich, they may choose where and how to live, and their choices in turn limit the options of the poor.

As a result, terms such as *individual freedom* and *equality of opportunity* may be meaningful for capitalists, but can are meaningless for working people, who must work for the capitalists if they are to survive. Socialism teaches that true freedom and true equality require social control of the resources that provide the basis for prosperity in any society. Karl Marx and Friedrich Engels made this point in *Manifesto of the Communist Party* (1848) when they proclaimed that in a socialist society "the condition for the free development of the individual is the free development of all."

According to an essay by Nicholas Buccola, from Frederick Nietzsche's perspective, the emergence of socialism as a moral and political ideal can be attributed to the first century, the Christian rejection of this world for life after death, and the moral perfectionism of Jean-Jacques Rousseau and other eighteenth century thinkers. In addition to these long-term factors, Nietzsche thought there were more immediate reasons for socialist challenges to the economic and political hierarchy.

First, Nietzsche thought those he called "socialist rabble" (political agitators) contributed to unrest by convincing workers that they should be dissatisfied with their lot in life. Nietzsche believed that the ruling class in industrial culture, those commonly referred to as capitalists, "lacked noble manners" and, as such, did not command sufficient respect from the working class. In Nietzsche's mind, these two factors played off one another and created the conditions necessary for revolutionary thought and action.

In his 1886 book titled *Beyond Good and Evil,* Nietzsche argues that "ordinary human beings," especially workers, "exist for service and the general advantage and may exist only for that." It does not follow that workers are mindless slaves that get nothing out of their existence. In his 1895 book titled The Anti-Christ, Nietzsche goes on to add that "their service is the only kind of happiness of which the great majority are capable."

Beyond the happiness attained in performing his particular task well, the workers also receive comfort in religion which gives an inestimable contentment with their situation and type, manifold peace of the heart, an ennobling of obedience, one further happiness and sorrow with their peers and something transfiguring and beautifying, something of a justification for the whole everyday character, the whole lowliness, the whole half-brutish poverty of their souls.

Perhaps nothing in religion is as revered as the pious teaching of even the lowliest of how to place themselves, through spirituality, in an imagined higher order of things and thus maintain their contentment with the reality that life on earth if difficult and meant to be so.

Plainly stated, Nietzsche believed the common worker is naturally suited for a simple, specialized existence in which he can find happiness in his role and comfort in the assurances of his religion. As previously noted, the smooth operation of society depends upon the contentment of the various classes. In Nietzsche's view, the average citizen can and should be content with their lot in life.

But this contentment is periodically disrupted by the socialist rabble, a socialist champion who undermine the citizenry's sense of satisfaction with his small existence who make him envious, who teach him revenge is necessary. Nietzsche viewed socialist agitators as a type of religious leaders of a new slave rebellion and the workers as the disenfranchised population that is waiting to be led by their noses.

The propaganda of the socialist agitator causes the worker to become dissatisfied by his lot in life and he begins to ask questions. A prime example might be something like:

why should "the boss" have a life that is so much more comfortable than my own? The propaganda of the socialist agitator is not, by itself, sufficient to bring about mass rebellion because the recognition that one is subordinate to someone else is not ostensibly a valid cause for discontent.

What matters is not that you are in a subordinate position, but who you are subordinate to. In his 1882 book, *The Gay Science*, Nietzsche explains that submission to powerful, frightening, even terrible persons, like tyrants and generals, is not experienced as so painful as is submission to unknown and uninteresting persons like politicians.

The manufacturers and entrepreneurs of business probably have been too lacking so far in all those forms and signs of nobility that alone make a person interesting. Due to the fact that many business owners, politicians, medical and legal professional lack an appreciation for the people on which they depend for revenue, it is not difficult to see how the average citizen gets the idea that it is only accident and luck that elevates one person above another, thus the seeds of socialism are planted.

The concepts of individual achievement and accountability are undermined by those who fail to demonstrate a lack of appreciation for the common citizen. By default, the arguments of the socialist agitator against individual entrepreneurship and private property ownership begin to seem more plausible. While private property seems to be the most divisive topic regarding socialism, not all socialist agree on what "property" should be owned collectively.

Some socialists believe that almost everything except personal items such as clothing should be public property. One example of this perspective is the type of communal society envisioned by Sir Thomas More in his Utopia (1516). More's vision had everyone living and working inside a walled community reminiscent of the days of feudalism where the citizenry worked the fields and factories in support of the community and its appointed leaders.

However, history has demonstrated that the idea that human beings are naturally good and that their goodness can be created or recovered by abolishing the right to own private property is altruistic nonsense.

Christianity and Platonism were combined in More's *Utopia*, which apparently recommends communal ownership as a way of controlling the sins of pride, envy, and greed. Land and houses are common property on More's imaginary island of Utopia, where everyone works for at least two years on the communal farms and people change houses every 10 years so that no one develops pride of possession. Money has been abolished, and people are free to take what they need from common storehouses. All the Utopians live simply, moreover, so that they are able to meet their needs with only a few hours of work a day, leaving the rest for leisure.

More's *Utopia* is not so much a blueprint for a socialist society as it is a commentary on the failings he perceived in the supposedly Christian societies of his day. Religious and political turmoil, however, soon inspired others to try to put utopian ideas into practice. Common ownership was one of the aims of the brief Anabaptist regime in the Westphalian city of Münster during the Protestant Reformation, and several communist or socialist sects sprang up in England in the wake of the Civil Wars (1642–51).

Chief among them was the Diggers, whose members claimed that God had created the world for people to share, not to divide and exploit for private profit. When they acted on this belief by digging and planting on land that was not legally theirs, they ran afoul of Oliver

Cromwell's Protectorate, which forcibly disbanded them. Other socialists, however, have been willing to accept or even welcome private ownership of farms, shops, and other small or medium-sized businesses that supported the community and its appointed leaders through taxation.

Another source of contention among socialists concerns the way in which society exercises its control of property and other resources. In this case the main camps consist of those typically defined as centralists and decentralists. Centralist socialists want to invest public control of property in a central authority, such as the state under the guidance of a political party or proletariat, as was the case in the Soviet Union. Conversely, decentralist socialists believe that decisions about the use of public property and resources should be made at the local, or lowest-possible, level by the people who will be most directly affected by those decisions.

The origins of socialism as a political movement lie in the Industrial Revolution. Its intellectual roots, however, reach back almost as far as recorded thought, even as far as Moses, according to one history of the subject. Socialist or communist ideas certainly play an important part in the ideas of the ancient Greek philosopher Plato, whose *Republic* depicts an austere society in which men and women of the guardian class share with each other not only their few material goods but also their spouses and children. Early Christian communities also practiced the sharing of goods and labor, a simple form of socialism subsequently followed in certain forms of monasticism. Several monastic orders continue these practices today.

Whether utopian or practical, these early visions of socialism were largely agrarian. This remained true as late as the French Revolution, when the journalist François-Noël Babeuf and other radicals complained that the Revolution had failed to fulfill the ideals of liberty, equality, and fraternity. Adherence to "the precious principle of equality," Babeuf argued, requires the abolition of private property and common enjoyment of the land and its fruits. Such beliefs led to his execution for conspiring to overthrow the government. The publicity that followed his trial and death, however, made him a hero to many in the 19th century who reacted against the emergence of industrial capitalism.

Conservatives who saw the settled life of agricultural society disrupted by the insistent demands of industrialism were as likely as their radical counterparts to be outraged by the self-interested competition of capitalists and the squalor of industrial cities. To their moral outrage at the conditions that were reducing many workers to pauperism, the radical critics of industrial capitalism added a faith in the power of people to put science and an understanding of history to work in the creation of a better form of society. The term *socialist* came into use about 1830 to describe these radicals, some of the most important of whom subsequently acquired the title of utopian socialists.

One of the first utopian socialists was the French aristocrat Claude-Henri de Saint-Simon. Saint-Simon did not call for public ownership of productive property, but he did advocate public control of property through central planning, in which scientists, industrialists, and engineers would anticipate social needs and direct the workers of society to meet them. Saint-Simon believed that history moves through a series of stages, each of which is marked by a particular arrangement of social classes and a set of dominant beliefs.

Thus, feudalism, with its landed nobility and monotheistic religion, had given way to industrialism, a complex form of society characterized by its reliance on science, reason, and the division of labor. In such circumstances, Saint-Simon argued, it makes sense to put the economic arrangements of society in the hands of its most knowledgeable and productive members, so that they may direct economic production for the benefit of all.

Another early socialist, and industrialist, Robert Owen, first attracted attention by operating textile mills that were both highly profitable and, by the standards of the day were remarkably humane. Meaning no children under age 10 were employed. Owen's fundamental belief was that human nature is not fixed but formed.

If people are selfish, depraved, or vicious, it is because social conditions have made them so. Change the conditions, he argued, and people will change. Teach them to live and work together in harmony, and they will do so. Thus, Owen set out in 1825 to establish a model socialist community. The community called New Harmony, was established in the state of Indiana, and was to be a self-sustaining cooperative community in which property was commonly owned. New Harmony failed within a few years, taking most of Owen's fortune with it.

Similarly, a wealthy French socialist named François-Marie-Charles Fourier believed that a free society breeds selfishness, deception, and other evils. Fourier believed that social institutions such as marriage, the male-dominated family, and the competitive market confine people to repetitive labor or a limited role in life and thus frustrate the need for variety. Accordingly, Fourier envisioned a form of society that would be more in keeping with human needs and desires.

Such a "phalanstery," as he called it, would be a largely self-sufficient community of about 1,600 people organized according to the principle of attractive labor, which holds that people will work voluntarily and happily if their work engages their talents and interests. All tasks become tiresome at some point, however, so each member of the phalanstery would have several occupations, moving from one to another as his interest waned and waxed. Fourier left room for private investment in his utopian community, but every member was to share in ownership, and inequality of wealth, though permitted, was to be limited.

Despite their imagination and dedication to the cause of the workers, none of the early socialists met with the full approval of Karl Marx, who is unquestionably the most often credited theorist of socialism. Marx and collaborator Friedrich Engels were primarily responsible for attaching the label "utopian," which they intended to be derogatory, to Saint-Simon, Fourier, and Owen, whose altruistic depictions of socialism they contrasted to their own "scientific" approach.

According to Marx, the path to socialism proceeds not through the establishment of model communities that set examples of harmonious cooperation to the world, but through the clash of social classes. A scientific understanding of history shows that these struggles will culminate in the triumph of the working class and the establishment of socialism.

The basic elements of Marx's theory are to be found in German philosophy, French socialism, and British economics. Of these, German philosophy was surely the formative influence on Marx's thinking. Marx was a philosophy student at the University of Berlin when the idealism of G.W.F. Hegel dominated German philosophy. Hegel maintained that history is the story of the unfolding or realization of "spirit," a process that requires struggle, agony, and the overcoming of obstacles to the attainment of self-knowledge.

Just as individual persons cannot realize their potential, especially the potential for freedom, if they remain forever in a childish or adolescent condition, so spirit must develop throughout history in a dialectical fashion.

In other words, individuals and even nations are seen as characters in a drama that proceeds through the clash of opposing ideas and interests to a greater self-awareness and appreciation of freedom. Slavery, for example, was long taken for granted as a natural and acceptable practice, but the slave's struggle to be recognized as a person was bringing an end to slavery as master and slave came to recognize their common humanity and spirit, thereby curtailing the master's false sense of superiority.

Like Hegel, Marx understood history as the story of human labor and struggle. However, for Marx it was the story of struggles between classes over material or economic interests and resources. In place of Hegel's philosophical idealism, Marx developed a materialist or economic theory of history.

Before people can do anything else, he held, they must first produce what they need to survive, which is to say that they are subject to necessity. Freedom is therefore largely a matter of overcoming necessity. Necessity compels people to labor so that they may survive, and only those who are free from this compulsion will be free to develop their talents and potential.

This is why, throughout history, freedom has usually been restricted to members of the ruling class, who use their control of the land and other means of production to exploit the labor of the poor and subservient. The masters in slaveholding societies, the landowning aristocracy in feudal times, and the middle class who control the wealth in capitalist societies have all enjoyed various degrees of freedom, but they have done so at the expense of the slaves, serfs, and industrial workers, or proletarians, who have provided the necessary labor.

For Marx, capitalism is both a progressive force in history and an exploitative system that alienates capitalists and workers alike from their true humanity. It is progressive because it has made possible the industrial transformation of the world, thereby unleashing the productive power to free everyone from necessity. Yet it is exploitative in that capitalism condemns the proletarians, who own nothing but their labor, to lives of unending labor while enabling the capitalists to reap the profits.

This is a volatile situation, according to Marx, and its inevitable result will be a war that will end all class divisions. Under the pressure of depressions, recessions, and competition for jobs, the workers will become aware that they are being exploited. This awareness will encourage them to overthrow their rulers through spontaneous uprisings, seizing control of factories, mines, railroads, and other means of production, until they have gained control of the government and converted it into a revolutionary dictatorship of the proletariat.

Under socialism or communism, Marx nor Engels drew any clear distinction between the two, government itself will eventually atrophy as people gradually become less selfish and seek to share ownership of the means of production. Freed from necessity and exploitation, people will finally live in a true community that gives each individual the means of cultivating his gifts in all directions.

Marx maintained that the revolution by which socialism would be achieved was ordained by the logic of capitalism itself, as the capitalists' competition for profits led them to create their own opposition in the proletariat. Even the role of the revolutionary is largely symbolic. Socialist agitators can do no more than speed along the inevitable revolution and ease its birth pangs. This, at least, was Marx's more or less official position.

In his writings and political activities, however, he added several qualifications. He acknowledged, for example, that socialism might supplant capitalism peacefully in England, the United States, and other countries where the working class was gaining more control of its future. In short, Marx was not the inflexible economic determinist he is sometimes taken to be. But he was convinced that history was on the side of socialism and that the equal development of all people to be achieved under socialism would be the fulfillment of history.

While many prominent socialists were militant atheists, others expressly connected socialism to religion and sought to integrate Christian social teachings with modern science and industry to create a society that would provide for all basic human needs. In England, the Anglican clergymen Frederick Denison Maurice and Charles Kingsley initiated a Christian socialist movement at the end of the 1840s on the grounds that the competitive individualism of unrestricted capitalism was incompatible with the communal spirit of Christianity.

Although neither Christianity nor any other religion was a dominant force within socialist theory or politics, the connection between Christianity and socialism persisted through the 20th century. An example of this connection is the Christian Socialist Movement in Britain, which affiliates itself with the British Labor Party. Several members of Parliament have belonged to the Christian Socialist Movement, including Prime Minister Gordon Brown, the son of a Methodist minister, and his predecessor, Tony Blair, an Anglican who converted to Catholicism not long after he left office.

Next in the evolutionary tale of socialism is a version styled after the tactics of the Roman general Fabian Cunctator commonly referred to as Fabianism, emerged in Britain. Fabian the Delayer avoided pitched battles by gradually wearing down Hannibal's forces. Instead of revolution, the Fabians favored bringing about socialism gradually. Their notion of socialism entailed social control of property through an effectively and impartially administered state, a government of enlightened experts.

The Fabians themselves were mostly middle-class intellectuals, including George Bernard Shaw, Sidney and Beatrice Webb, Graham Wallas, and H.G. Wells, who thought that persuasion and education were more likely to lead to socialism than violent class warfare. Rather than form their own political party or work through trade unions, the Fabians aimed at gaining influence within existing parties. They eventually exercised considerable influence within Britain's Labor Party, though they had little to do with its formation in the early 1900s.

Near the anarcho-communists on the decentralist side of socialism were the syndicalists. Syndicalism developed at the end of the 19th century out of the French trade-union movement. It was a significant force in Italy and Spain in the early 20th century until it was crushed by the fascist regimes in those countries. In the United States, syndicalism appeared in the guise of the Industrial Workers of the World, or "Wobblies," founded in 1905.

The hallmarks of syndicalism were workers' control and direct action. Syndicalists distrusted both the state, which they regarded as an agent of capitalism, and political parties, which they thought were incapable of achieving radical change. Their aim was to replace capitalism and the state with a loose federation of local workers' groups, which they meant to bring about through direct action such as a general strike of workers that would bring down the government as it brought the economy to a halt.

Georges Sorel elaborated on this idea in his 1908 book titled *Reflections on Violence*, Sorel regarded the general strike not as the inevitable result of social developments but as a myth that could lead to the overthrow of capitalism if only enough people could be inspired to act on it.

Related to syndicalism but nearer to Fabianism in its reformist tactics, Guild Socialism was an English movement that attracted a modest following in the first two decades of the 20th century. Inspired by the medieval guild, an association of craftsmen who determined their own working conditions and activities, theorists such as Samuel G. Hobson and G.D.H. Cole advocated the public ownership of industries and their organization into guilds, each of which would be under the democratic control of its trade union.

The role of the state was less clear: some guild socialists envisioned it as a coordinator of the guilds' activities, while others held that its functions should be limited to protection or policing. In general, however, the guild socialists were less inclined to invest power in the state than were their Fabian compatriots. Revisionist Eduard Bernstein, an associate of Engels, was also exposed to the Fabians while living in England. Their example encouraged him to question aspects of Marx's theory.

Like others, Bernstein observed that the living and working conditions of the proletariat were not growing more desperate, as Marx had predicted, but were in fact improving, largely as a result of trade-union activity and the extension of the franchise. This led him to conclude that the revolutionary overthrow of capitalism was neither necessary nor desirable. In his 1899 book titled *Evolutionary Socialism*, he argued for a gradual, peaceful transformation to socialism, noting that it would be safer than the revolutionary route, with its dangerously vague and potentially tyrannical dictatorship of the proletariat.

Bernstein's writings drew a swift and hostile reaction from his SPD comrades, and from revolutionary Marxists elsewhere. After several years of polemical war between revisionists and orthodox Marxists, the revisionists eventually triumphed within the SPD, which gradually abandoned its revolutionary pretenses. Nevertheless, some proponents, such as Rosa Luxemburg, remained faithful to the spirit of revolutionary Marxism.

Among the remaining orthodox Marxists was a Russian revolutionary V.I. Ulyanov, better known by his pseudonym Lenin. As the leader of the Bolshevik faction of the Russian Social-Democratic Workers' Party, Lenin himself had been accused of straying from the Marxist path. The problem for Russian Marxists was that Russia in the late 19th century remained a semifeudal country with barely the beginnings of industrial capitalism.

To be sure, Marx had allowed that it might be possible for a country such as Russia to move directly from feudalism to socialism, but the standard position among Marxists was that capitalism was a necessary stage of economic and historical development; otherwise, there would be neither the productive power to overcome necessity nor the revolutionary proletariat to win freedom for all as it emancipated itself from capitalist exploitation.

While this had been the standard position among Russian Marxists, it was not Lenin's. Lenin had little faith in the revolutionary potential of the proletariat. He believed that workers would fight only for better wages and working conditions, and therefore needed to be educated, enlightened, and led to revolution by professional revolutionaries. Moreover, the authoritarian nature of the

Russian government required that revolutionaries be conspiratorial, disciplined, and elitist.

World War I proved to be a watershed in the history of socialism. In the years before war broke out, most European socialists had held that the only war the proletariat should fight was the class war against the bourgeoisie. When the war began, however, socialists were forced to choose between international socialism and their countries, and they generally chose the latter—though there were notable exceptions, Luxemburg and Lenin among them. Once the SPD's contingent in the Reichstag voted to issue war credits, socialists in other countries fell into line behind their own governments.

World War I also inflicted severe hardships on the Russian people, thereby contributing to the collapse of the tsarist regime and creating an opportunity for revolution, which the Bolsheviks seized in the Russian Revolution of 1917. Lenin's standing among revolutionary Marxists soared, though Luxemburg and others deplored the way in which the dictatorship of the proletariat was becoming a dictatorship of the All-Russian Communist Party, as the Bolsheviks named themselves in 1918.

Still, the communists' victory gave Luxemburg and other revolutionaries hope that the Russian example would inspire socialist revolutions elsewhere. For his part, Lenin feared that his regime could not survive without the aid of socialist neighbors. Accordingly, he called a meeting in Moscow to establish a Communist International, or Comintern.

The response from other countries was tepid, and, by the time the delegates convened in March 1919, the prospects for a new international had been further dimmed by the failure of the Spartacus Revolt of the new Communist Party of Germany. Lenin pressed on with the formation of the Comintern, but it was soon apparent that it was an agent of the new Union of Soviet Socialist Republics (the U.S.S.R. was formally created in 1922) and not of international socialism as such. Indeed, by this time a fissure had clearly developed between communists on the one hand and socialists, or social democrats, on the other.

The division took institutional form as revolutionary Marxists adopted what came to be called Marxism-Leninism. The socialists, known as social democrats, were a more diverse group, including both revisionists and non-Marxists, but they were united in their commitment to peaceful, democratic tactics. They were also less likely than the communists to claim that history was moving inexorably toward the demise of capitalism and more likely to appeal to ethical considerations.

On the communist side, the standard was set by the increasingly totalitarian regime of Joseph Stalin in the Soviet Union. Following the typical evolution of socialism, Lenin's death in 1924 led to a power struggle between Stalin and Leon Trotsky. Stalin not only won the struggle but eventually ordered the deaths of Trotsky and other rivals, as well as millions more who opposed or resisted his policies.

While professing to be a revolutionary in the Marxist-Leninist tradition, Stalin concentrated his efforts on building socialism in one country, largely through a program of forced collectivization and industrialization.   Fascist oppression was also a major problem for socialists in other countries such as Italy under Mussolini, Spain under Franco, and Germany under Hitler.

Socialist parties had drawn enough votes in Germany, Britain, and France to participate in or even to lead coalition governments in the 1920s and '30s. However, wherever fascists power dominates, communists and socialists were among the first to be suppressed. In the

U.S., Eugene V. Debs won nearly one million votes in the U.S. presidential election of 1920. However, his showing represented less than 4 percent of the votes cast and remains the electoral high point for American socialists.

After World War II, the ensuing Cold War deepened the fracture between communists and other socialists who referred to themselves as democrats, were opposed to the one-party rule of the Soviet Union. The Labor Party, for example, won a parliamentary majority in the British elections of 1945 and subsequently established a national health care system and public control of major industries and utilities; when the party lost its majority in 1951, it peacefully relinquished the offices of government to the Conservatives.

The communists also claimed to be democrats, but their notion of social democracy rested on the belief that the people were not capable of governing themselves. In the case of China in 1949, Mao declared that the new People's Republic of China was to be a "people's democratic dictatorship." CCP would rule in the interests of the people by suppressing their enemies and building socialism. Freedom of expression and political competition were bourgeois, counterrevolutionary ideas. This later became the justification for one-party rule by other communist regimes in North Korea, Vietnam, Cuba, and elsewhere.

Throughout Europe the socialist parties were modifying their positions and enjoying frequent electoral success. The Scandinavian socialists set the example of mixed economies that combined largely private ownership with government direction of the economy and substantial welfare programs, and other socialist parties followed suit. Even the Social Democratic Party of Germany dropped its Marxist pretenses and committed itself to a social market economy.

Although some welcomed this blurring of boundaries between socialism and welfare-state liberalism as a positive sign, the more radical student left of the 1960s complained that there was little choice between capitalism, the communism of the Marxist-Leninists, and the bureaucratic socialism of western Europe.

In practice, most new kinds of socialism typically combined appeals to indigenous traditions, such as communal land ownership, with the Marxist-Leninist model of one-party rule for the purpose of rapid modernization. In Tanzania, for example, Julius Nyerere developed an egalitarian program that collectivized village farmlands and attempted, unsuccessfully, to achieve economic self-sufficiency under the guidance of a one-party state. In Asia, no distinctive form of socialism emerged.

Aside from the communist regimes, Japan was the only country in which a socialist party gained a sizable and enduring following, to the point of occasionally controlling the government or participating in a governing coalition. Nor has there been a peculiarly Latin American contribution to socialist theory. The regime of Fidel Castro in Cuba tended to follow the Marxist-Leninist path in the 1950s and '60s, though with increasing moderation in later years, especially after the collapse of the Soviet Union in 1991.

Liberation theology called on Christians to give priority to the needs of the poor, but it has not developed an explicitly socialist program. Perhaps the most distinctively Latin American expression of socialist impulses was Venezuelan Pres. Hugo Chávez's call for a Bolivarian Revolution. However, Chávez did not establish a connection between his version of socialism and Bolívar's thoughts and deeds.

In many ways, the attempt by Salvador Allende to unite Marxists and other reformers in a socialist reconstruction of Chile is most representative of the direction that Latin American socialists have taken since the late 20th century. Elected by a plurality vote in a three-way election in 1970, Allende tried to nationalize foreign corporations and redistribute land and wealth to the poor. These efforts provoked domestic and foreign opposition, which led to a military coup and Allende's death.

Beginning in the late 20th century, the advent of what many considered a postindustrial economy raised doubts about the relevance of socialism, which was in theory and in practice primarily a response to industrial capitalism. This conviction led to much talk of a "third way" that is, a democratic socialism position that would preserve the socialist commitment to equality and welfare while abandoning class-based politics and public ownership of the means of production.

However, in 1995 the British Labor Party under Tony Blair embraced the third way by forsaking its long-standing commitment to the nationalization of basic industries; in general elections two years later, the Labor Party won a landslide victory, and Blair served as prime minister for the next 10 years. Other heads of government who professed the third way in the 1990s included Bill Clinton of the U.S., Chancellor Gerhard Schröder of Germany, and Prime Minister Wim Kok of the Netherlands.

Critics on the left complained that the third way reduced equality to an equal chance to compete in economies in which the rich were growing ever richer and the poor were increasingly disadvantaged. Such a position, they insisted, is hardly socialist. Democratic socialism is increasingly referred to as "market socialism" in an attempt to make socialism more palatable.

As the name implies, market socialism blends elements of a free-market economy with social ownership and control of property. Proposals have varied, but the basic idea is that businesses will compete for profits, as in capitalism, but they will be owned, or at least governed, by those who work in them. The workers in every business will choose their supervisors, control their working conditions, set the prices of their products, and decide how to share the profits or losses of their enterprise. Market socialism is being promoted as a form of workplace democracy that enables workers not only to vote in political contests but also to have a say in the economic decisions that affect them daily in their work.

Market socialism does not represent the world that Marx and his followers envisioned as the fulfillment of history. But it does promise to promote cooperation and solidarity rather than competitive individualism, and it aims at reducing, if not eliminating, the class divisions that foster exploitation and alienation. In these respects, this modest, decentralized version of socialism continues to sound the themes that have long inspired people to take up the cause of socialism.

Even in Latin America and other places where socialists continue to call for direct, public ownership of natural resources and major industries, they nevertheless leave room for private competition for profits in the marketplace. In one way or another, socialists now seem more interested in bringing the free market under control than in eliminating it completely.

Chapter 2

The Appeal of Democratic Socialism

One of the alleged reasons for the recent shift in public opinion toward socialism was the Great Recession of 2008. A combination of crushing student loan debt, low wage jobs and escalating home and rental costs has a huge impact on Millennials and Generation Z'ers. The vast numbers of which pursued general liberal arts degrees rather than developing specialized skills that generally would set them up for good paying jobs upon graduation. Therefore, many millennials favor some form of socialism in order to level the economic playing field.

However, socialist ideology does not originate within the minds of individuals, rather it is created and taught by small groups in the political class that use the common worker as an instrument in their own quest for power. Thanks to the media's deep connections to Congress, various government personnel, and political agendas, the recession was portrayed as a catastrophic failure of the current president and government leaders.

Millennials and recent college graduates who came up being taught that they should get a trophy simply because they were on the team, most of whom had never held a job for more than two years at that time or owned a profitable business, bought into the narrative of socialists like Bernie Sanders who preached that capitalism was the source of all their problems and who sent them looking for alternatives. Many of them, especially younger Americans, found it in a "soft socialism" that was part welfare state, part administrative state, part socialist democracy.

The siren song of democratic socialism is alluring. Perhaps it is human nature that we want to be taken care of in all circumstances and be assured that no other person has material circumstances much better than our own. But the record is crystal clear. Socialism, the preaching of moral collectivism in service to one's individual ego leads to underperforming economies, loss of individual opportunity for generations, equality implemented by everyone being poor except the political leaders, lack of innovation and progress, and incredible political and religious oppression.

A recent poll by YouGov reported that given a choice, 44 percent of young people between the ages of 16 and 29 would prefer to live in a socialist nation rather than a capitalist country and that another seven percent would choose communism. One might ask, then why haven't they moved to one of the many socialist countries? My guess would be, and the same poll revealed, because only 33 percent of the respondents could correctly define socialism as based on the common ownership of economic and social systems as well as the state control of the means of production.

What most millennials perceive as "socialism" seems to be a mix of government funded entitlements and a welfare state. They want to keep the high-level consumerism culture that free markets provide, while at the same time correcting perceived social ills infecting our country. The idea of wealth redistribution is particularly attractive to students who do not have much to redistribute, but it is interesting given the right set of circumstances how quickly they abandon the concept.

For example, when students are given the analogy of sharing GPA points from those at the top of the class with those at the bottom, many react negatively to the idea, especially if they have worked hard to achieve their grades.

Those with lower grades who stand to benefit are more open to the idea. In other words, democratic socialism is attractive where people are drawn to the entitlements that the system brings, whether the entitlements are for them or others, as long as the system does not negatively affect them. Little thought is given to the coercion and force required to implement the well-intentioned policies or the potential unintended consequences.

Many up and coming political leaders hold up Sweden and Denmark of examples of how the U.S. should operate. However, both Sweden and Denmark favor free markets and private rather than government ownership of their major industries. Also not addressed by the democratic socialist is that Danish domestic spending including comprehensive health care is funded by a personal income tax of 57 percent.

The millennial trend toward an acceptance of socialism is not new. A 2014 poll by Reason-Rupe, a libertarian group, reported that 58 percent of those aged 18 to 24 had a favorable view of socialism. A 2018 Gallup survey found that while 51 percent of Americans age 18-29 had a positive image of socialism, 90 percent were favorable to entrepreneurship, while 78 percent favored free enterprise. How can a group be 55 percent socialist and 78 per cent entrepreneurial?

My first thought is that these less-than-enlightened people are products of the American public education systems. That by age 29, someone could spend on average 25 years in the public education system and be so ignorant of world, or even American, history is both fascinating and appalling at the same time.

A May 2020 article by Samuel Arnold, titled *What Is Democratic Socialism and Why is it Growing More Popular in the U.S.?* the suggestion is made that democratic socialism only seeks control of the Fortune 500 companies like Walmart, Apple, Microsoft, Pfizer, Merck, AEP, etc. But then in the same paragraph states, "Socialists don't want to collectivize your toothbrush, your iPhone, or your Nintendo Switch." I wonder where they buy their stuff.

One has to wonder if these same millennials choose socialism, if in exchange for free education and free health care, they would have to give up their personal property, such as their smart phones or credit cards? Would seven percent of millennials still declare their willingness to live under communism if they knew the real costs of communism as practiced in some 40 nations over the past century?

How would they react to the denial of free speech, a free press, and free assembly, the imprisonment and execution of dissidents, no free and open elections, no independent judiciary or rule of law, the dictatorship of the Democratic Socialist Party in all matters and on all occasions? Maybe I digress.

The modern day standard bearer for democratic socialists is Bernie Sanders. The senator from Vermont captured the hearts and the votes of many millennials with his call for single payer health care, free public college, campaign finance reform, and racial, economic, and climate justice. The prime target of his hostility is the top one percent in America who own, it is true, some 40 percent of the nation's total wealth — as much as the bottom 90 percent.

What Bernie and other socialist rarely point out is that the same top one percent pay 40 percent of the individual income taxes. Sanders had a ready explanation for how to pay for all of the freebies: increase the taxes on the rich and their corporations. In Bernie's world, there is such a thing as a free lunch because the bill will be paid by those at the top.

It does not seem to matter to millennials that Sanders never started a business or even held a legitimate job until he was elected to Congress well into middle age and that he now owns three upscale homes paid for by American taxpayers. Or that while portraying himself as a freelance journalist, he published rape fantasies such as "A woman enjoys intercourse with her man as she fantasizes about being raped by three men simultaneously."

Sanders also wrote that "The manner in which you bring up your daughter with regard to sexual attitudes may very well determine whether or not she will develop breast cancer." Apparently, the man is an authority on female sexuality and health. While he may be the best ideologue for democratic socialism, I am not sure he is the best representative for distributed wealth and social equality.

The most dramatic proof of socialism's new-found political clout was the election of Alexandria Ocasio-Cortez who promised Medicare for all, free college tuition, legalization of marijuana, the elimination of the U.S. Immigration and Customs Enforcement, and that the world as we know it would end in twelve years. Alexandria Ocasio-Cortez represents a breed of democratic socialists who want to expand individual freedom, create a society where everyone has a real say in the major decisions affecting their lives, and to decommodify basic necessities like health care, education, and housing.

In political economics, decommodification is the social entitlements plank in the campaign platform of most democratic socialists often touted as and the peoples' freedom from market dependency. A typical example is the socialist ideal that one can chose to leave the labor market with little or no loss of income. However, this ideal clashes with the fact that social democracy has the goal of high labor force participation.

Efforts to resolve this paradox have revealed that employment *impeding* policies did not come social democracy institutions. After all, the credited founder of socialism, Karl Marx and the Communist Manifesto states "that if a man doesn't work, he shall not eat."

Socialists also want the provision of health care, choices about who receives healthcare, to be a government provided, single payer system, free of charge to all people. Similarly, programs like universal social housing, and free public college would not only help people live more dignified lives, they would free people up to choose what kind of work they wanted to do, and empower them to stand up to bad bosses or simply quit.

Socialists, democratic or otherwise, believe that businesses should be run collectively and democratically by their workers. "Socialism," explains a member of Democratic Socialists of America's national steering committee, "is the democratization of all areas of life, including but not limited to the economy." The people who produce goods and services should decide their work hours and conditions, not have them dictated by owners.

Democratic socialists also want control over major social decisions put in the hands of workers, consumers, and anyone else who might be affected. In the immediate term, that means exploitation of the main stream and social media and removing institutional barriers to popular rule (such as the Electoral College and the Senate in the United States).

Additionally, democratic socialism will require socializing the financial sector, so that investment priorities will be set by the public instead of private account managers. It will mean nationalizing our energy and transportation systems allegedly to break our dependence on fossil fuels and prevent the worst effects of capitalist-created climate change. Eventually, most major industries will need to be brought under public control, to eliminate capitalists' ability to control pro-worker policies by withholding investment. Contrary to millennial beliefs, these are not new proposals.

Recently, socialism has been likened to a pseudo-religion grounded in pseudo-science and enforced by political tyranny masquerading as a pseudo-constitutional government. Proponents of democratic socialism or any other kind of socialism fail or simply refuse to acknowledge that much of what they enjoy in life are the fruits of capitalism and would quickly be taken away by the very style of government they want implemented.

As mentioned earlier, according to the DSA, socialists seek to convert industries like health care into public utilities; regulate coal mines out of existence; subsidize sectors of the economy like solar energy; and operate corporations like Amtrak and Freddie Mac, and present socialism as the only reasonable alternative to the unchecked greed of capitalism. However, as the democratic socialist movement grows in numbers and influence, how will its leaders resolve the discrepancy between pure socialism and the soft socialism of popular opinion.

Socialism purists seek public ownership of the means of production as well as centralized control of goods and services. Soft socialists see a limited role for the private sector. Will socialist politicians be able to fuse the two ideals of socialism like conservative politicians blended traditional conservatism and libertarianism in the 1960s and 1970s? The realities of socialism are incomprehensible to those who have never heard of the Berlin Wall, the Gulag, the killing fields of Cambodia, the Tiananmen Square massacre, or the daily bread lines in Moscow. But then, modern socialists do not agree that these were actually socialist states.

Chapter 3

How Capitalism Is Perceived by Socialists

When those who hold negative views of capitalism are asked why they hold this view, about 23 percent of respondents say that capitalism creates an unfair economic structure, echoing a common sentiment among socialists that capitalism only benefits a small number of people or that wealth in this country is unfairly distributed.

Similarly, 20 percent of self-identified socialists believe that capitalism has an exploitative and corrupt nature, often harming either people or the environment. Additionally, eight percent of Americans with negative views of capitalism believe that corporations and wealthy people undermine the democratic process by having too much power in political matters.

According to the DSA and other proponents of socialism, capitalism is an economic system where a small group of people own what Marx called the "means of production" the land, buildings, machines, and raw materials necessary to produce useful things. The vast majority (workers) do not.

Workers have to sell their labor to businesses for a wage, and the business owner(s) directs them to produce certain goods, which are then sold on the market. After paying wages and purchasing whatever else they need to replenish the means of production, businesses keep a share of the revenue they make as profits.

On the surface, relations between workers and business owners are free and equal. Allegedly, workers voluntarily sell their labor to employers and can bargain for a higher wage or turn down their boss's offer. But even a cursory reflection reveals that most workers are not really free to rebuff their employer: the vast majority of people must work in order to obtain life's necessities. If they do not, they will go without food, housing, clothing, medicine, and other things necessary for a decent life. In theory, workers could simply look for a better employer.

However, many workers do not have the time and ability to seek out a better job. Taking time off may mean missing a rent payment or being unable to feed one's family. And even if workers do have the flexibility to look for better offers, they are unlikely to find any. Businesses compete with each other for market share and to maximize profits, so every firm tries to get as much work out of its employees for as little money as possible.

Unless a worker is lucky enough to have rare or especially valued skills, they will face a host of equally dismal job offers from stingy employers. Employers, on the other hand, benefit from having a massive pool of unemployed or underemployed workers, many willing to accept whatever they can get. The threat of starvation forces workers to seek employment; once employed, they spend most of their waking hours under the boss's domination. That is why radicals have long described the plight of the worker as one of wage slavery.

Capitalists loom large even in the lives of those who do not work for them. Business owners and investors unilaterally decide whether to continue production or move a factory or office abroad and force the rest of us to live with the consequences. Pharmaceutical companies refuse to develop desperately needed antibiotics and antiviral medicines. Real estate investors evict and displace working-class residents from their neighborhoods so they can build luxury condos.

The most dramatic example of capitalists deciding everyone else's fate is climate change: a handful of fossil-fuel companies are sending us careening toward crisis. Rather than fostering democracy, capitalism is a system where a handful of billionaires and CEOs are allowed to imperil the planet in order to ensure healthy returns on their investments.

Socialism, democratic or otherwise, espouses the doctrine that capitalism necessarily involves an absence of democratic control and a lack of freedom for the vast majority of people and point to what they call fundamental myths to support these associations. One is that workers always have the freedom to quit their job or find a new one. Defenders of capitalism also often insist that workers who want better jobs can improve their situation through acquiring new skills. But this retort ignores reality, too.

While Americans have long cherished the idea that the United States is a land of equal opportunity and unparalleled social mobility, whether a person graduates high school or can attend a top college is largely a function of race and class. And what kind of job a person ends up with is largely shaped by what jobs their parents had.

Another sustaining myth is that, while capitalists may enjoy immense economic power, they do not have inordinate political power. "One person, one vote" gives everyone an equal say in shaping society through democratic elections. Pay attention to contemporary politics for just a moment, and you will see that this is a lie. Far from a neutral arbiter of competing ideas or interests, liberal democratic states systematically support the business class over the working class.

There are three main reasons for this. One is that most elected officials and top bureaucrats are drawn from the ranks of the ruling class, and so are most likely to adopt the worldview and promote the interests of that class. Another is that capitalists can use their wealth to wield massive financial power over the state. They hire armies of lobbyists to influence legislators, use their ownership of media to shape the public narrative, and purchase loyalty through huge campaign donations. If you are rich enough, you can use your personal fortune to buy your way to public office (or at least put yourself in contention).

It is natural to think there is something deeply unfree about work in the contemporary United States. That feeling is connected to a real material fact about the workplace: one of the defining features of the employment relationship in all capitalist countries is that the worker's will is, by law, subordinate to the employers. The employer has the right, within broad bounds, to define the nature of the task, who performs it, and how. This shows up in all kinds of surveillance, control, and forced submission, commonly known as maximizing productivity and extracting profit.

Just consider who controls one of the body's most essential functions: going to the bathroom. Workers in the United States can be forced to urinate during employer-mandated drug testing; or forbidden from urinating if it is not break time.

In Amazon warehouses for example, workers whose every move is tracked, forego trips to the restroom to avoid being disciplined or fired for too much "time off task." Employers control or seek to control many other aspects of workers' lives, from their Facebook posts and political speech to the wages they earn and the rates at which they work.

It is no surprise, then, that there is a long history of comparing capitalist wage labor to slavery. In 1873, Ira Steward, son of abolitionists and founder of the eight-hours movement, looked out over the United States' industrial sweatshops, its fourteen-hour days for poverty wages, and wrote, "Something of slavery still remains." His point was not that wage labor and slavery were the same, but that, for all the talk of emancipation, many aspects of the employment relationship smacked more of servitude than of freedom.

By the time Steward wrote those words, the critique of wage slavery was at least fifty years old. Another often cited passage was written in 1828 by Thomas Skidmore, avowed critic of slavery and founder of the New York Working Men's Party, wrote:

For he, in all countries is a slave, who must work more for another than that other must work for him. It does not matter how this state of things is brought about; whether the sword of victory hew down the liberty of the captive, and thus compel him to labor for his conqueror, or whether the sword of want extort our consent, as it were, to a voluntary slavery, through a denial to us of the materials of nature.

A significant topic that socialists seldom discuss is that not everyone decrying wage slavery did so on egalitarian grounds. In the early republic, some racist white workers invoked wage slavery not to argue against chattel slavery and wage labor together but, instead, to maintain that white workers should not be reduced to the condition of black people.

Theophilus Fisk, for instance, worried in the 1830s about "the white slaves of the North" but denounced abolition. Freedom was, for racist figures like Fisk, a racial privilege rather than a universal end. It was possible, then, to object to wage slavery as "white slavery" and to use the term to divide people by race, rather than to unite them in class struggle. But that was generally the less common use of the term.

A common refrain of socialism on the topic of wage slavery as a reflection of capitalism is that the whole process of civilization has been to emancipate human beings from the conditions of slavery in which they have been held by their fellow men. Civilization has not yet reached its highest point of development, nor can it develop much further without first having abolished wages slavery, for that form of slavery stands to-day as one of the greatest barriers to the progress of civilization.

Socialist typically define capitalism in terms of oppression, exploitation, and economic inequality. Capitalism is frequently criticized for establishing power in the hands of a minority capitalist class that exists through the exploitation of a working class majority; for prioritizing profit over social good, natural resources and the environment; and for being an engine of economic inequality and market instability.

Modern socialists believe that capitalism is an attack on personal integrity that undermines individual freedom and hold that workers should own and control their workplace. Many socialists argue that large-scale voluntary associations should manage industrial manufacture while workers retain rights to the individual products of their labor.

As such, they see a distinction between the concepts of private property and personal possession. Whereas private property grants an individual exclusive control over a thing whether it is in use or not and regardless of its productive capacity, possession grants no rights to things that are not in use.

Socialists argue that the accumulation of capital generates waste through externalities that require costly corrective regulatory measures. They also point out that this process generates wasteful industries and practices that exist only to generate sufficient demand for products to be sold at a profit (such as Google's algorithm based advertisement), thereby creating rather than satisfying economic demand.

Similarly, capitalism promotes what socialists view as irrational activity, such as the purchasing of commodities only to sell at a later time when their price appreciates (known as speculation), rather than for consumption. Therefore, a crucial criticism often made by socialists is that making money, or accumulation of capital, does not correspond to the satisfaction of demand (the production of use-values). The fundamental criterion for economic activity in capitalism is the accumulation of capital for reinvestment in production.

In socialist ideology, private property relations viewed as restraints on the potential of productive forces in the economy. According to socialists, private property becomes obsolete when concentrated in centralized, social institutions based on private appropriation of revenue until the role of the capitalist becomes redundant.

With no need for capital accumulation and a class of owners, private ownership or control of the means of production is perceived as being an outdated form of economic organization that should be replaced by a free association of individuals based on public or common ownership of these socialized assets.

Private ownership imposes constraints on planning, leading to uncoordinated economic decisions that result in business fluctuations, unemployment, and a tremendous waste of material resources during crisis of overproduction. Eco-socialists criticize capitalism as inefficient and wasteful.

They note a shift from pre-industrial reuse and thriftiness before capitalism to a consumer-based economy that pushes ready-made materials. In the process, social-ecologists say, capitalism has created a profit driven system based on selling as many products as possible.

Planned obsolescence has also been criticized as a wasteful practice under capitalism. By designing products to wear out faster than need be, new consumption is generated. Critics believe this practice only benefits corporations by increasing sales while at the same time generating excessive waste. A well-known example is the charge that Apple designed its iPod to fail after 18 months.

Many Marxist economists argue that the system of perpetual capital accumulation leads to irrational outcomes and a mis-allocation of resources as industries and jobs are created for the sake of making money as opposed to satisfying actual demands and need.

Likeminded critics argue that capitalism leads to the unfair distribution of wealth and power; a tendency toward market monopoly or government imperialism, counter-revolutionary wars and various forms of economic and cultural exploitation, repression of workers, and other phenomena such as social alienation.

Capitalism is regarded by many socialists to be irrational in that production and the direction of the economy are unplanned, creating many inconsistencies and internal contradictions and thus should be controlled through public policy.

In the United States, socialist critics of capitalism, such as Ravi Batra, argue that the capitalist system has inherent biases favoring those who already possess greater resources. The inequality may be propagated through inheritance and economic policy. Rich people are in a position to give their children a better education and inherited wealth and that this creates large differences in wealth between people who differ in ability or effort.

One study shows that in the United States 43.35% of the people in the *Forbes* magazine "400 richest individuals" list were already rich enough at birth to qualify. Another study indicated that in the United States wealth, race and schooling are important to the inheritance of economic status, but that IQ is not a major contributor and the genetic transmission of IQ is even less important. Batra has argued that the tax and benefit legislation in the United States since the Reagan presidency has contributed greatly to the inequalities and economic problems and should be repealed.

Many socialists, traditional and modern, believe that the emphasis on and constitutional protection of private property is the problem. Socialists seem to think that private property leads to despotism, owning property gives one the right to use and manipulate others. By default, private property means the monopoly of wealth, the right to prevent others using it, whether the owner needs it or not.

In the past, some socialists have sought to replace ownership of private property with a system where people can lay claim to things based on personal use and claiming that "private property is the domination of an individual, or a coalition of individuals, over things; it is not the claim of any person or persons to the use of things" and "this is, usufruct, the right to enjoy the use and advantages of another's property short of the destruction or waste of its substance.

Social mutualists support markets and private property, but not in their present form. They argue that particular aspects of modern capitalism violate the ability of individuals to trade in the absence of coercion. Mutualists support markets and private property in the product of labor, but only when these markets guarantee that workers will realize for themselves the value of their labor.

In recent times, most economies have extended private property rights to include such things as patents and copyrights. Critics see this as coercive against those with few prior resources. They argue that such regulations discourage the sharing of ideas and encourage nonproductive behavior, both of which contribute to a prohibitive barrier to entry into the market. Not all pro-capitalists support the concept of copyrights, but those who do argue that compensation to the creator is necessary as an incentive.

One of the modern criticisms to the sustainability of capitalism is related to the so-called commodity chains, or production/consumption chains. These terms refer to the network of transfers of materials and commodities that is currently part of the functioning of the global capitalist system.

Examples include high tech commodities produced in countries with low average wages by multinational firms and then being sold in distant high income countries; materials and resources being extracted in some countries, turned into finished products in some others and sold as commodities in further ones; and countries exchanging with each other the same kind of commodities for the sake of consumers' choice. According to critics, such processes, all of which produce pollution and waste of resources, are an integral part of the functioning of capitalism.

And finally, a team of Finnish scientists hired by the UN Secretary-General to aid the 2019 Global Sustainable Development Report assert that capitalism as it exists today is failing, primarily because it focuses on short term profits and fails to look after the long term needs of people and the environment.

Their report goes on to link many seemingly disparate contemporary crises to this system, including environmental factors such as global warming and accelerated species extinctions and also societal factors such as rising economic inequality, unemployment, sluggish economic growth, rising debt levels, and impuissant governments unable to deal with these problems. The scientists say a new economic model, one which focuses on sustainability and efficiency and not profit and growth, will be needed as decades of robust economic growth driven by abundant resources and cheap energy is rapidly coming to a close.

Chapter 4

Democratic Socialism-Not About Freedom

According to an article by Neal Meyer of *Jacobin Magazine*, democratic socialism is about *expanding* freedom and democracy — liberating us from the tyranny that permeates everyday life under capitalism. Meyer also suggests that democratic-socialism has nothing to do with authoritarian rule. But then he also notes that the perception that democratic socialism leads to tyranny is "given credence by the fact that many twentieth-century governments that claimed the mantle of socialism were repressive regimes."

It is often argued that socialism is a secular version of Christianity, referring to Acts 2-5, which describes the early Christians as having "all things in common." It is true that following Pentecost, Christians sold their possessions and property and shared the results with "any that might have need."

But there is a critical distinction between Christians and socialists. Jesus urged his followers to give up *their* possessions while socialists want to give away the possessions of *others.* The Apostle Paul is sometimes quoted as saying that "money is the root of all evil." What he actually wrote in a letter to Timothy was that "*love of* money is the root of all kinds of evil." His warning was of an unhealthy attachment to money, not about the currency itself.

In *The Communist Manifesto* Marx says, "The theory of the communists may be summed up in the single sentence: Abolition of private property." He knew that depriving individuals of this basic freedom would not be easy and that dictatorship by the proletariat — and violence — would be required. The abolition of private property is necessary, Marx argued, because it is the central cause of the perennial clash between the classes.

But then as now private property is not just any right; it is integral to civilization. There never was a time or place when all possessions were collectively owned. There is no convincing evidence, writes the Harvard historian Richard Pipes, that there were societies that knew "no boundary posts and fences" or ignored "mine" and "thine."

In *The Constitution of Liberty*, Nobel Laureate Friedrich Hayek writes that "the recognition of private property is an essential condition for the prevention of coercion." He quotes Lord Acton as saying that "a people averse to the institution of private property is without the first element of freedom" and Henry Maine as asserting: "Nobody is at liberty to attack [private] property and to say at the same time that he values civilization. The history of the two cannot be disentangled."

Generally speaking, socialism stands in direct contrast with Christian theology with its idea of a fixed human nature infuriated Marx, who was not just an atheist but a God-hater who denounced religion as "the opium of the masses." His disciples, led by Lenin, always targeted the churches when they came to power. They initiated without apology a campaign of terror, shutting down churches, executing priests and bishops and violating nuns. The horrors were justified as part of the capitalist class-cleansing Marx envisioned.

The Founders of the American Revolution rejected those who believed that man was born without any imprint and sided with those who accepted that man was born in the image of God. As the Declaration of Independence states, all men "are endowed by their Creator with certain unalienable rights." The Founders disagreed with those who thought man was perfectible and instead took the Christian position that man's nature was fallen.

As Madison famously observed, "If men were angels there would be no need for government" and "ambition must be made to counteract ambition." It is a reflection of human nature, Madison said, that "such devices should be necessary to control the abuses of government." George Washington summed up the Founders' realism: "We must take human nature as we find it, perfection falls not to the share of mortals."

Without exception, every socialist leader from Vladimir Lenin to Fidel Castro promised to initiate basic political freedoms such as free elections, a free press, and free assembly. None of them fulfilled those promises. The American journalist Louis Fisher, once an enthusiastic chronicler of Soviet economic advances, recounted how much the Soviet Union had changed: "Ubiquitous fear, amply justified by terror, had killed revolt, silenced protest, and destroyed civil courage. In place of idealism, cynical safety-first propaganda. In place of dedication, pursuit of personal aggrandizement. In place of living spirit, dead conformism, bureaucratic formalism, and the parroting of false clichés."

As it was in the Soviet Union under Stalin; so it has been in every socialist experiment since the Bolshevik Revolution of 1917. The Soviet-Nazi agreement was the cracking point for many intellectuals in the West, including the American Louis Fisher, who accused Stalin of building an imperialistic militaristic system in which he is, and his successor will be, "the Supreme Slave Master." How then, Fisher asked, can anyone interested in the welfare of people and the peace and progress of humanity support such a system?

Democratic socialism is described in textbooks as "a political philosophy that advocates for political democracy alongside a socially owned economy with a particular emphasis on workers' self-management and democratic control of economic institutions within market socialism."

A distressing number of today's college students are being lured by socialism's siren song. This trend demonstrates a triumph of misplaced social justice idealism over individual freedom. We can lay blame at the feet of far too many of today's college professors, ensconced in academia and lacking real world experience

Democratic socialists such as Bernie Sanders want total control of the economy even though hardly any of them have ever started, run, or sold a business of any size or importance. They view free enterprise and wealth accumulation for successful rich people to be inherently "evil."

Robert Heilbroner, author of "The Worldly Philosophers," acknowledged that individual freedom is "directly opposed to the basic socialist commitment to a deliberately embraced collective moral goal." If the word "collective" sounds familiar it may be because it was the driving principle of socialism under Joseph Stalin who killed millions establishing collectives in the 1930s as did Mao in the 1950s.

Heilbroner also recognized that establishing the socialist economic ideal requires massive intervention and planning in politics and culture when he said, "Indeed, that is what planning means. Command by planning need not, of course, be totalitarian. But an aspect of authoritarianism resides inextricably in all planning systems. A plan is meaningless if it is not carried out, or if it can be ignored or defied at will." Socialists are authoritarians by definition.

Socialism has always faced "two historic problems. The first is the necessity to intervene deeply, and decisively, into the economy in order to establish the socialist order in the first place. The second is the need to continue a policy of painful intervention to accommodate the socialist economy, once set in place." A clear recent example of how democratic socialist policies are typically put in place and the enforced is the Affordable Care Act.

Socialism, then and now, is a massive social engineering experiment that, to be successful, must develop a new society of individuals devoid of their selfish tendencies. This inescapably leads to restricting individual freedom. Sigmund Freud identified what he referred to as the central defect in socialist doctrine.

Socialism is based on the idea that private property is the primary source of human immorality. This foundational belief says that mankind can be redeemed only if the institution of private property were abolished and replaced by a kinder and more humane system.

Utopian socialist Robert Owen believed "the character is formed *for,* and not *by,* the individual, the adoption of socialist principles of truth will enable mankind to prevent, in the rising generation, almost all of the evils and miseries which we and our forefathers have experienced."

Heilbroner goes on to explain that socialists are frequently hostile when their policies are questioned, "Because socialist society aspires to be a good society, all its decisions and opinions are inescapably invested with moral import.

Every disagreement with them, every argument for alternative policies, and every nay-saying voice therefore raises into question the moral validity of the existing government, not merely its competence." Anyone opposing a socialist government is by definition opposing the collective good and must be dealt with, in Heilbroner's word, "ruthlessly" as an example to other potential dissidents.

Democratic socialist would have us believe that its roots are in love and fraternity rather than revenge and aggression. According to Freud, "It is always possible to bind together a considerable number of people in love, so long as there are other people left over to receive the manifestations of their aggressiveness." Socialists, like other underprivileged human beings, express their instinct for power by declaring war on those they deem responsible for their suffering.

Nietzsche says, "it is a basic error to think of socialists, or any other herd morality, as a collectivity with collective aims." Rather, he contends, goals exist in "single individuals" and the "herd is a means, and no more." Like Freud, Nietzsche held that the driving motivation in socialism is *not* a love for one's fellow man, but rather a love of power and a desire to find the most effective way to exercise one's delusional and predatory nature on others.

Another unexpected source of opposition to socialism is apparently American Civil Liberties Union managing editor Matthew Harwood when he explains that "the collective, undergirded by the power of the state, will always triumph over the messiness of individuals' liberty to think, speak, write, work, and associate as they wish." This fact is reportedly an inconvenient truth most democratic socialist just sweep under the rug.

Harwood then asks some excellent questions like, "Could democratic socialists abide a free press, one where the media criticize the party for its economic illiberalism? Could writers and artists critical of the regime work without fear of political repression and surveillance? "Could citizens of the United States rest assured that democratic socialists would peacefully relinquish the reins of government to a party they deem 'capitalistic' if they lose the next election when their goal is to abolish capitalism?"

Democratic socialism is an economic and cultural configuration that suppresses if not eliminates the market economy and the alienating and selfish culture it produces. As Heilbroner reluctantly acknowledged, socialist planning cannot co-exist with individual rights. Instead, under socialism, culture must produce some form of commitment to the idea of a moral collectivism.

American culture, devoted to the sovereignty of the individual, naturally asserts the rights of individuals to speak their minds freely, to act as they wish within reasonable grounds, to behave as John Stuart Mill preached in his treatise *On Liberty*. A socialist culture, Heilbroner stated, could not abide this "celebration of individualism" because it is "directly opposed to the basic socialist commitment to a deliberately embraced collective moral goal."

However, today's democratic socialists argue that under democratic socialism, individual civil and political rights, which are routinely violated, would be strengthened, and public resources would be devoted to the development of a genuinely free press and a democratically-administered mass media. Several hundred years of human history say otherwise.

Freedom in a Democratic Republic goes hand-in-hand with freedom in the marketplace. Individual freedom allows people to start with nothing but an idea and sometimes turn it into a multibillion-dollar international corporation. Socialism does not allow such massive private business successes.

There has not been one single company started in socialist France since 1975 that has grown to be worth more than one billion dollars. By comparison, Apple, Amazon, and

Microsoft, all started in the U.S. since 1980, and are worth one trillion dollars each in market capitalization, making thousands of employees and all early shareholders very wealthy people.

Democrats have been courting socialism throughout history and for the entirety of the 21st century. Democrats have an avowed socialist, Bernie Sanders, leading the way for their government take over. Elizabeth Warren can spout off socialist doctrine with the best of them. Failed candidate Pete Buttigieg's father was an outspoken defender of a "modern version" of Marxism as a professor at Notre Dame.

There is no "modern version" of Marxism that is tolerable to the freedoms we enjoy in our modern American Democratic Republic. Democratic socialism is incompatible with the foundational principles of American freedom that have empowered the individual over the state since 1789.

It sounds good to promise free college tuition, free health care, free housing, free phones, and even free money the way U.S. representatives Rashida Tlaib, Alexandria Ocasio-Cortez and Ilhan Abdullahi Omar have been. The only problem is, who will pay for it? When you run out of other people's money through wealth redistribution and taxation, then what? That is when the ruling government takes over all aspects of life, as has happened throughout history.

Socialist authority means control of any dissent against it. Therefore, free speech will be nullified. It is ironic that the very people demanding a turn to socialism will become its own victim. As much as they use our First Amendment to foster socialism, free speech is the first freedom that is lost because socialist regimes cannot allow a disobedient populace to rise up against its authority.

After the loss of free speech, so goes other freedoms such as the ability to defend yourself, or own a gun, practice a religion, or assemble a protest. The loss of the pursuit of happiness, and ultimately the loss of our Constitutional government and freedom itself all become the casualties of socialism.

The United States is not a country that thrives because of big government welfare programs and government control. It thrives because its citizens know that hard work is rewarded, freedom is protected, and individuals can enjoy the fruits of their labor as they see fit. It is that dream of personal freedom and individual property that has defined America as the land of opportunity.

Chapter 5

Social Conditioning

More than any other issue, race has divided American society. In a June 2020 article for *The Washington Times*, Aubry Shines recounts historical records regarding both the Republican and Democrat party positions on the issue of race. The professionally written article summarizes various political attempts to improve race relations and the long-standing pattern of oppressive manipulation of minority social-identity groups by one party more so than the other.

Within the Democratic party there exist a group of elitists self-identified as Democratic Socialists. A major focus of this group is identity politics. The indoctrination and manipulation of self-styled victim groups is the long-standing social conditioning agenda of Democratic Socialism.

And every election cycle, Democrats trot out the same rhetoric and make the same empty promises that they've been making for over a century. This repetitive cycle constitutes social conditioning. When the U.S. general election puts democrats in control, the only significant changes are in the personal wealth of the politicians.

Historically, through the established psychological process of operant conditioning, the Democratic Party has diligently worked to convince Black-Americans and the mélange of other victim groups that they simply cannot survive in America without the help of democrat and socialist politicians to promote the groups' agenda. The recent efforts to erase and rewrite history through intimidation and violence is simply par for the course.

The very foundation of socialism relies on repetition over time to convince identity based demographics that they are persecuted, and that only a Democratic Socialist mayor, governor, congressperson or president will be able give them a chance. Twenty-first century identity politics demand public persecution and ridicule of anyone who has ever said or written anything negative toward any minority group.

Social conditioning occurs when classical and operant conditioning techniques are combined to stereotype social identity groups such as Blacks, gays, Hispanics, and others through systematic association with negative events and anti-social attitudes.

Some examples were alluded to earlier in the chapter on cultural differences. Unkept communities are associated with poverty. Poverty is often associated with unemployment. High unemployment rates are generally associated with criminal activity, therefore unkept communities are associated with criminal activity, and so on.

In the U.S. today, non-compliance with popular opinion, particularly regarding minority identity groups, has been associated with racism and intolerance by the media so frequently that disagreeing with popular opinion is now is tantamount to a felony conviction. No amount of public apology, penance, groveling, or rehabilitation will suffice. Once you have been accused, you, your family, and any close associates are guilty, period.

In attempts to placate minority groups and gain social approval employees are being summarily fired, executives are being removed from their positions, students are being expelled or refused admission all because of a comment, Facebook post, or tweet made years ago.

Unless of course, you are a registered socialist or major donor to the Democratic Party, in which case the racist sins of your past are forgotten long before they become an issue.

Meanwhile, co-conspirators in the media, the MSM, BLM, Antifa, and other Democratic Party affiliates, selectively edit film clips, alter transcripts of speeches, and do all they can to create the illusion that opponents of Democratic Socialism are all racists. The public who blindly accept the Democratic Socialists mantra without question have become the useful idiots of our time.

In the context of social conditioning, several minority based identity groups have been deployed to help shape public opinion and identify dissenters. One such identity group is Black Lives Matter (BLM).

Thirty-two percent of Blacks Americans are skeptical overall that the country will eventually make the changes needed to bring about racial equality. Among those blacks who think change will eventually come, only 23% say Black Lives Matter will be effective in helping bring about equality, while 34% of whites believe the group will be effective in helping bring about equality for Black Americans.

Social conditioning is clearly demonstrated among BLM supporters in that Young white adults are more enthusiastic about Black Lives Matter than middle-aged and older whites. Sixty percent of those ages 18 to 29 say they support BLM, compared with 25% of whites ages 50 and older. Young whites are also somewhat more likely than their older counterparts to say that the Black Lives Matter movement will be at least somewhat effective in the long run.

Political views on Black Lives Matter also differ significantly by party identification. Sixty four percent of Democrats support BLM, while 42% of Republicans and Independents say they support the movement. White Democrats are also much more likely than Republicans and independents to say that the movement will ultimately be at least somewhat effective in bringing about racial equality.

These statistics are not unusual when one considers the correlation between Marxist philosophy and the stated mission of the BLM movement. According to the founders of BLM:

"*We are a collective of liberators who believe in an inclusive and spacious movement. We also believe that in order to win and bring as many people with us along the way, we must move beyond the narrow nationalism that is all too prevalent in Black communities. We must ensure we are building a movement that brings all of us to the front.*

We affirm the lives of Black queer and trans folks, disabled folks, undocumented folks, folks with records, women, and all Black lives along the gender spectrum. Our network centers those who have been marginalized within Black liberation movements.

We are working for a world where Black lives are no longer systematically targeted for demise.

We affirm our humanity, our contributions to this society, and our resilience in the face of deadly oppression.

Similarly, Marxism is based on the perspective that;

"Society does not consist of individuals, but expresses the sum of interrelations, the relations within which these individuals stand compared to others in their social group." *The history of all hitherto existing society is the history of class struggles. Freeman and slave, patrician and plebeian, lord and serf, guild-master and journeyman, in a word, oppressor and oppressed, stood in constant opposition to one another, carried on uninterrupted, now hidden, now open fight, a fight that each time ended either in a revolutionary reconstitution of society at large, or in the common ruin of the contending classes."*

I would like to reiterate here that the essential defining aspect of democracy is the existence of competitive and fair elections; an element which emphasizes diversity of opinion and serves to place one group in power, while relegating the others to dissent. The diversity inherent to democratic systems instills in a country's citizens an awareness of difference, which theoretically propagates more tolerant individuals.

However, with autocratic identity-based groups like BLM as in political regimes such as Democratic Socialism, expression of diversity is restrained, being considered the basis of disorder and thereby detrimental to the state. This is why when well-meaning supporters of racial equality express their sincere belief that "all lives matter," they are immediately attacked those who demand to be recognized as different. Is this not the basic definition of racism?

Generally speaking, in democratic societies, freedom of expression and speech and a free media are widely accepted principles. Political parties and social groups in democratic societies are therefore able to express varied and opposing opinions on societal concerns, and such opinions are broadcast to large swaths of the population.

For most individuals, this exposure to diversity promotes tolerance of difference. While diversity tends to breed tolerance, there is a critical exception to this generality. When human beings are continuously subjected to negative input such as the chronic "*Breaking News*" and melodramatic reporting of seemingly rampant violence everywhere and the futility of escape, the human psyche is repeatedly pushed into the "fight or flight" mode. When individuals are exposed to diversity under constant aversive conditions, they become less tolerant of difference.

Another example is arrival of the SARS-CoV-2, the causative source of Covid-19 that prompted politicians across the world government spectrum to summarily shut down the global economy. Democrats, and their handlers, in the U.S immediately used it as an opportunity to manipulate minority identity groups like BLM and Antifa to harass and publicly ridicule a duly elected president who, being a political outsider, is viciously hated by Democrats and some Republicans simply because he is not one of their own.

The elitist Democrats across the nation continued to receive their full salaries and benefits while almost completely destroying the U.S. economy through fearmongering, social conformity requirements, and mandating business closures. Through the imposition of quarantine measures "for the good of everyone" politicians, not scientist, took control and eliminated the private business sector's ability to earn a living and support their families outside of government provided welfare.

To divert attention from their overreach, government officials, through complicit media outlets, incessantly focused the public's attention on episodes of police and racist violence, minority group oppression, and other go-to distractions during election cycles. The most glaring example of this is the exploitation of the death of George Floyd by the media and the U.S. Democratic Party.

Never before has the death of a convicted felon and street thug meant so much to so many. It is likely Floyd's death and the accompanying social unrest would have been just another social minority injustice added to a long list, except that several up and coming Socialists are up for re-election in 2020, as well as the outsider American president.

George Christie, writing in *The Daily News*, summarizes the recent events nicely when he says, "The economic damaged from the resulting stock market slide, cancellation of venues, government-mandated restrictions on citizen's participation in their daily lives and the near-nuclear reaction of fear and negativity from the Democrat media and their directors in Washington is the mushroom of fallout that has created havoc and panic countrywide."

The Democrats' goal is only to destroy Donald Trump, and they care little for those who fall in that path. I don't recall such panic for all of the previous 18 coronaviruses, but I do continue to see the Democrat biased mainstream media use the virus existence to further erode our founders' visions establishing the greatest country in the world.

The immediacy of the public's compliance and submission to the dramatic fearmongering encouraged elected Democrat officials and other prominent Socialists to continue issuing executive orders, city or county ordinances, and corporate directives to maintain control of subordinates until independent thinkers and other dissidents learn to comply with what was immediately characterized as "the new normal."

Chapter 6

How Socialism Leads to Tyranny

There is plenty of anecdotal evidence that both socialism and communism lead to tyranny. Most advocates for democratic socialism will say it is somehow different from traditional socialism and cannot be properly explained or defined by historical precedents even as recent as 2010. Democratic socialists try to soften what their ideas would look like in reality and sidestep the endless historical and present examples of the ideology's failure.

The typical defense is along the lines of "all other socialist leaders were corrupt and incompetent leaders who lacked the sincerity, virtue, and wisdom to regulate the day-to-day affairs of their citizens." However, the fact remains that regardless of it place on the timeline, government produces nothing and therefore cannot give you anything that it does not first take away from someone else. And what it gives, it can easily take away.

Bernie Sanders was recently asked by a Russian immigrant and student from the University of Michigan how his brand of democratic socialism would be different than the kind that led to the horrors of the USSR. "What happened and existed in the Soviet Union was not socialism. It was authoritarian communism," Sanders replied. "And communism, whether in Cuba, whether in the Soviet Union, or whether in other countries, was marked by totalitarianism, was marked by throwing millions of people into the Gulag."

The Gulag, the Soviets' infamous network of prison camps, held as many as 17 million political prisoners in the

1930s and 1940s, many convicted based on false testimony.

National Review's David Harsanyi wrote about why this is an absurd way to look at socialism as an idea. He noted that it's true not every socialism system leads to absolute economic collapse and dictatorship. For instance, Israel's early socialist experiments, Harsanyi explained, merely kept people poor, not starving.

Although socialists see things such as private property rights as suspicious, a tool for the rich to exploit the weak, nearly the opposite is true. Strict private property rights are a protection for the weak against the strong, a protection against the mob as well as the elite, powerful, and connected.

Harsanyi added, "Leftists like Bernie like to act as if socialist ideology is incompatible with totalitarianism when the opposite is true. The nationalization of industry and dispensing with property rights can't be instituted without coercion and a centralized authoritarian effort. And even if the effort to redistribute property is first supported by the majority, as soon the state comes for your stuff—and it always does—the 'democratic' part of the equation starts to dissipate.

In the most basic sense, the distinction between the outcomes of these systems comes down to an understanding of human nature. The Founding Fathers were deeply concerned with placing limitations on power to protect the equal and natural rights of citizens and create a free and functioning country.

A socialist society can't rely on strict limitations on government power, as a free society is inherently, materially unequal. Left to pursue their own goals, people of various abilities and motivations will invariably achieve different outcomes. Even the general desire to "pursue happiness" as each of us sees it typically will end with highly varied outcomes.

No collective system, no matter how crafted, can make up for the individual variances of our lives. Socialism is the tool that leftists dream will smooth over inequality, will lift up the oppressed to put them on equal footing with the privileged.

To fulfill its promises, socialism must inherently be authoritarian. To get people to fork over their wealth, force citizens to make up for economic shortages detached from the variance of supply and demand, and ensure that nobody rises too much or falls too low, a powerful, compulsive, and ultimately unlimited government is necessary.

The problem is, unlimited power in the hands of a monarch, a mob, or a central committee always will be prone to rampant abuse and will sacrifice the God-given rights that are the very foundation of a just government. Not only is freedom sacrificed but perhaps ironically, so is community, as society devolves to seeing the blunt instrument of the state rather than family and civil society as the basis of well-being.

So although socialists, or democratic socialists, or whatever they like to call themselves, continually dance around or dismiss the evidence that so many socialist countries have devolved into dictatorship, the reality is that authoritarianism is the foundation of the socialist system, not an anomaly.

The good news is, at least in the U.S., you are entitled to housing, education, health care, and food. But that does not mean people no longer have to work. The real issue that needs to be addressed here is that a government that controls everything can quash dissent by changing the economic situation of anyone who is pointing out their defects or is involved with the opposition.

Under socialist rule, if you write an insightful article about how a local government official is making a huge mistake, you may find your assigned tenement changed to the worst one available in a city where you do not want to live. If you question something your supervisor directs you to do, you may find yourself reassigned from the job you trained years to get to one "more in line with the common good."

When most of us interface with the outside world, we expect the highest possible pay for the work we do, and when we buy things, we expect the highest quality at the lowest possible price. Economics adds up those personal tendencies over millions of people in large, complex societies and comes up with a few simple rules that describe economic behavior.

Supply and demand, marginal revenue and marginal cost, the theory of money, and specialization and exchange are really just simple rules that take all people's actions and abilities into account and arrive at a solution that balances the overall societal equation.

Socialists don't like these simple economic rules and come up with their own, such as "from each according to his ability, to each according to his needs," which conflicts with human nature. When you implement policies that conflict with human nature, you have to use force to implement them.

Every person who works in a socialist society is paid by the government and knows they will be paid whether the organization they are working for provides goods or services to customers or not. This is quite different than a society where most companies are private and employees know that if the company they work for does not sell products that pay the companies expenses, they won't be employed anymore.

The DSA has stated that people do not only work to avoid starvation or to satisfy their greed. "People enjoy their work if it is meaningful and enhances their lives. They work out of a sense of responsibility to their community and society. Although a long-term goal of socialism is to eliminate all but the most enjoyable kinds of labor, we recognize that unappealing jobs will long remain.

These tasks would be spread among as many people as possible rather than distributed on the basis of class, race, ethnicity, or gender, as they are under capitalism. And this undesirable work should be among the best, not the least, rewarded work within the economy.

For now, the burden should be placed on the employer to make work desirable by raising wages, offering benefits, and improving the work environment. In short, we believe that a combination of social, economic, and moral incentives will motivate people to work."

Let us look back at how that philosophy worked for Franklin D. Roosevelt. Capitalizing on the "progressive" policies of Woodrow Wilson, FDR declared on January 11, 1944 that it was time for the United States to adopt a Second Bill of Rights. These new "rights" included a "useful and remunerative job"; the opportunity to earn enough to provide "adequate" food clothing and recreation; to a "decent home" for his family; to "adequate" medical care; to a "good" education; and finally to "adequate" protection in old age and retirement. Interestingly enough, Roosevelt did not define what he meant by "adequate."

And now one can see why socialists Bernie Sanders, Alexandria Ocasio-Cortez, Omar, Tlaib and other Democrats are so enthusiastic about the Green New Deal. They can snuggle in comfortably with the Democratic Party and further their socialist agenda while truthfully claiming wide support from the Democrats political base.

Still not sure? Let's take a look at the Democratic Party's platform. It calls for a shorter work day, a guaranteed wage, public works, or infrastructure, programs to create jobs, guaranteed pensions for the elderly, unemployment insurance, a graduated or progressive income tax, and inheritance tax, capital gains tax, elimination of the Electoral College, and revision of the Constitution.

This list is nearly a mirror image of the Socialist platform since 1912. Just in case more clarification is needed, when the DSA was recently asked, "Aren't you a party that's in competition with the Democratic Party for votes and support?

The answer was immediate and clear, "No, we are not a separate party. Like our friends and allies in the feminist, labor, civil rights, religious, and community organizing movements, many of us have been active in the Democratic Party. We work with those movements to strengthen the party's left wing, represented by the Congressional Progressive Caucus. The process and structure of American elections seriously hurts third party efforts. Winner-take-all elections instead of proportional representation, rigorous party qualification requirements that vary from state to state, a presidential instead of a parliamentary system, and the two-party monopoly on political power have doomed third party efforts."

Then adding, "We hope that at some point in the future, in coalition with our allies, an alternative "national party" will be viable. For now, we will continue to support progressives who have a real chance at winning elections, which usually means left-wing Democrats." Those of us who have be around more than four decades, and who were taught world history, remember an organization formed in Germany based on these same ideals. Back then it was called the National Socialist Workers' Party.

Socialism is often a precursor of communism. Democratic Socialists believe in nationalizing some industries and or important societal functions but not all. They will usually nationalize utilities, transportation, and large industries that tend to have labor problems.

Here, the personalities involved matter a lot. Socialist governments either respect the prior governmental rules of free elections, separation of powers, and individual choice, or they push for complete government control of everything by their political party and end up allowing no dissenting political parties or individuals.

To understand whether socialism leads to communism, we should consider Great Britain after WWII, when socialist parties were elected to national political office, and Venezuela, where Hugo Chavez was elected president in 1999 on a socialist platform.

These post-war British socialists took it pretty seriously. They nationalized coal, electricity, steel, and the railways and set up the National Health Service to provide government-run health care. Farms and grocery stores were allowed to be private, and the British electoral system was left to allow free and fair elections.

After a number of years, the British economy performed too poorly under socialism to sustain the nation and the British people elected politicians who believed in free enterprise and turned things around. Socialism doesn't always have to lead to communism, and Britain pulled back from the brink when they saw that the socialist promise led to everyone being worse off.

In Venezuela, the democratically elected Chavistas (supporters of Hugo Chavez) pushed for governmental control and immediately brought in Cuban intelligence agents to assist them in quashing dissent, controlling the population, forcing businesses to sell goods and services at a loss, implement draconian currency controls, and were then surprised when the businesses stopped operating.

The result in Venezuela was that stores had no goods on their shelves, hospitals had no medicines or machines that worked, and ordinary people took to looking through trash for food. Various political maneuvers were implemented by the Chavistas, the legislature was restructured, the judiciary was stacked, and the electoral system was compromised.

As of 2020, any political avenue for changing the government in Venezuela is gone, and they have the very dictatorship that characterizes communist societies, along with a broken economy that works very poorly, even by communist standards. In Venezuela, the socialists pushed their way through to dictatorship and tyranny, and a complete social economic breakdown was the result.

Most politicians will use the power at their disposal to protect their own interests first. For socialism to work, a socialist government must control almost every personal, educational, political, and economic aspect of society. Once the communist party in any given country has command over almost every control point, they all seem to have enough competence to use that authority to stay in power.

I can think of very few cases where "the people" overthrew a communist government. When a communist government moves on to a more open, pluralistic society, it is almost always because the people at the top decide communism is a bad idea and it is time to move on.

A typical example of communist economics is the Soviet farm collectivization of the 1930s. All the private, family-owned farms of the Soviet Union were converted to large collectivized farms. Stalin privately admitted to Churchill that 10 million people died, either from starvation or resistance to the forced farm collectivization. With a communist dictatorship, when a leader goes off the rails, there are no moderating forces that bring compromise or allow negotiation for alternative paths to lead a society toward its goals.

A communist society's productivity is a mere fraction of the productivity of an economy based on capitalism and free enterprise. The work ethic deteriorated so severely in the Soviet Union that a saying began circulating among the workers: "They pretend to pay us, and we pretend to work."

For a society to operate at an economic level much lower than its potential for generations is a loss that can never be regained. One great defender of liberty in the United States that never gets much credit is your local police department. They enforce the laws we all care about—murder, assault, robbery—but they report no higher than the local mayor or county supervisor and are paid for by local taxes.

Communist societies are very top-heavy. They all have national-level police departments with ominous-sounding names that enforce the one true ideology over the entire country. In many communist countries, these national-level police forces turn family members against each other by asking children to turn in their parents if they say or do something against the government. One phone call seals your fate if you are a dissenter or independent thinker who is questioning how the government is doing things.

Conversely, imagine some high-level government official in a free society like in the United States said another political party needed to be eradicated by force and/or locked up in prison. They'd have to get the law passed and then get thousands of local police departments to enforce it—a daunting task. Decentralized power is a power that defends liberty.

Chapter 7

Capitalism in the United States

Capitalism, the free market economy, or the free enterprise system is an economic system dominant in the Western world since the breakup of feudalism, in which most means of production are privately owned and production is guided and income distributed largely through the operation of markets.

Capitalism has been getting a lot of attention lately through Democrats reminding people that some individuals are doing very well with capitalism and that the vast majority of us haven't been as successful as them. A system that rewards some people more than others may strike you as inherently unfair. Competitive capitalism, where some people try and fail and businesses go bankrupt and have to lay off their employees, seems stressful and unnecessary to some.

The establishment of capitalism in the U.S. was a major consideration in the Declaration of Independence. While the continuous development of capitalism as a system dates only from the 16th century, antecedents of capitalist institutions existed in the ancient world, and flourishing pockets of capitalism were present during the later European Middle Ages. The development of capitalism was spearheaded by the growth of the English cloth industry during the 16th, 17th, and 18th centuries.

The feature of this development that distinguished capitalism from previous systems was the use of accumulated capital to enlarge productive capacity rather than to invest in economically unproductive enterprises, such as pyramids and cathedrals. This characteristic was encouraged by several historical events.

Events and perspectives developed during the the Protestant Reformation of the 16th century encouraged public disdain for the avaricious accumulation of wealth, while hard work and frugality were given stronger religious sanction. Economic inequality was justified on the grounds that the wealthy were more virtuous than the poor.

Another contributing factor was the increase in Europe's supply of precious metal and the subsequent inflation in prices. However, wages did not rise as fast as prices in this period, and the main beneficiaries of the inflation were the capitalists. The early capitalists (1500–1750) also enjoyed the benefits of the rise of strong national states during the mercantilist era.

The policies of national power followed by these states succeeded in providing the basic social conditions, such as uniform monetary systems and legal codes, necessary for economic development and eventually made possible the shift from public to private initiative.

Beginning in the 18th century in England, the beginning of the industrial revolution, the accumulation of capital in the preceding centuries was invested in the practical application of technical knowledge during the Industrial Revolution. The ideology of classical capitalism was expressed in *An Inquiry into the Nature and Causes of the Wealth of Nations* (1776), by economist Adam Smith, which recommended leaving economic decisions to the free play of self-regulating market forces.

After the French Revolution and the Napoleonic Wars had put feudalism to rest, Smith's policies were increasingly put into practice. The policies of 19th-century political liberalism included free trade, national currency based on the gold standard, balanced budgets, and minimum levels of poor relief. The growth of industrial capitalism and the development of the factory system in the 19th century also created a vast new class of industrial workers whose generally miserable conditions inspired the revolutionary philosophy of Karl Marx.

World War I marked a turning point in the development of capitalism. After the war, international markets contracted, the gold standard was abandoned in favor of managed fiat currencies, banking power passed from Europe to the United States, and trade barriers multiplied. The Great Depression of the 1930s brought the policy of noninterference by the state in economic matters to an end in most countries and for a time created sympathy for socialism among many intellectuals, writers, artists, and, especially in western Europe, workers and middle-class professionals.

In the decades immediately following World War II, the economies of the major capitalist countries, all of which had adopted some version of the welfare state, performed well, restoring some of the confidence in the capitalist system that had been lost in the 1930s. Beginning in the 1970s, however, rapid increases in economic inequality within individual countries, revived doubts among some people about the long-term viability of the system.

Then following the financial crisis of 2007–09 and the financial recession that accompanied it, there was renewed interest in socialism among many people in the United States, especially persons born in the 1980s or '90s, a group that had been particularly hard-hit by the recession. Polls conducted during 2010–18 found that a slight majority of millennials held a positive view of socialism and that support for socialism had increased in every age group except those aged 65 or older.

It should be noted, however, that the policies actually favored by such groups differed little in their scope and purpose from the New Deal regulatory and social-welfare programs of the 1930s and hardly amounted to orthodox socialism.

For now, rather than focusing on who has and who has not, perhaps we would be better served to consider the things in our lives that make life more convenient if not better. Think about the idea that capitalism puts life-saving, game-changing, incredibly convenient products and services in your life whether you participate directly in working on those innovations or not. Thomas Edison would likely be extremely impressed with of your ability to instantaneously communicate with people thousands of miles away.

In the past, very rich and powerful people had to watch relatives die if they got certain kinds of bacterial infections. Now, you can easily go out and procure antibiotics. The richest person in Rome couldn't have his or her favorite perishable dish until their servants prepared it, and now you simply take your favorite dish out of the refrigerator and put it in the microwave. Progress has become so profound and pervasive that some are arguing that the average person in today's advanced countries wouldn't trade places with a billionaire 100 years ago.

It is important to mention that successful innovation yields very high societal returns. A successful innovation improves the lives of every human being using that innovation for the rest of humanity. Someone invented the wheel, and now billions of people have driven vehicles that use that wheel.

The person who invented malaria pills that would have kept President Teddy Roosevelt from getting the disease benefited all those hundreds of millions of people who will live in or travel to tropical zones where malaria is a problem.

I would argue that if an innovator lives a little better lifestyle than the rest of us during their lifetime, that's a small price to pay for all the future advantages their innovation brings to humanity.   And by the way, not all innovators are fabulously wealthy people.

Capitalism is very good at rewarding progress, and over time, a great deal of progress has been accomplished by capitalism. Some accomplishments of capitalism are game-changing, such as vaccines and the commercialization of the internet. Some innovations are more humble, such as the successful start-up of a restaurant with a good location or the right cuisine in a medium-sized town.

All around you, people are paying attention and trying to improve our world in ways big and small. Hundreds of years ago, someone invented a flathead screw for joining wood or metal together. In your lifetime, an impact driver was invented that now makes it easy to drive that screw with a handheld tool, and this process has replaced most nails.

Disk drives used to be the size of a rugby ball, and you placed those drives into a device the size of a washing machine. Now you can hold the storage of a thousand of those drives in a smartphone in the palm of your hand. All this progress makes products and services cheaper for all income groups in society, not just the wealthy.

Capitalism is responsible for almost all global progress. Socialist and communist societies have historically struggled with innovation in every realm except the military, Lasik procedure and the Rubik's cube. The Lasik procedure was developed because someone cut their eye in a bar fight in the Soviet Union, and a doctor was paying attention. The Rubik's cube was invented in Eastern Europe but commercialized in the West.

Capitalism involves many individuals, small businesses, and corporations working on ways to improve the lives of everyone on the planet. The good ideas rise to the top, while the bad ideas fail. Those resources quickly go elsewhere. The probability that a huge government bureaucracy with competing agendas could pick the successful ideas out of thousands of candidates and implement them to the customers that want them is laughable.

All this happens naturally and easily in a capitalist system. Ask yourself how long the world would wait for the smartphone if Cuba or North Korea had been relied upon to invent it.

Chapter 8

Personal and Fiscal Responsibility

It's easy to understand why people are emotionally drawn to the ideals of socialism. It draws its fundamental motivational source from a primary compassion. That is always there in human beings, and so that proclivity for sensitivity to that political message will never go away.

A key element of socialist indoctrination is the belief that an individual should no longer be seen as separate from the state, and that, through the absolute responsibility of the state over every facet of our lives, no issue is without a political cause.

Socialist believe strongly in state intervention. People are not expected to handle issues themselves. Any personal issue, any conflict between individuals, or any discomfort in life is no longer seen as something an individual should solve or endure. Instead daily life becomes an issue for the state to resolve through sweeping regulation.

It's through this ongoing process of crisis and response that the powers of government replace the powers of the individual. It results in regulations that slowly replace traditions of self-reliance with the tyranny of socialism.

The true nature of Socialism is often misunderstood as being simply an economic system, a belief in sharing, or an alternative to capitalism. Yet none of these are true. Socialism, as Karl Marx and others envisioned, was merely the initial developmental stage of communism. It's where the state has seized control of the means of production and the mechanisms of power and uses these to drive society toward the final goals of communism: the destruction of morality, tradition, family, and all individual social structures.

Socialism does not end at the control of business and finance. It is also a cultural, social, and atheistic ideology that looks to seize and dominate these aspects in each individual through the promotion of distrust of fellow citizens. It's because of socialist ideals that we have things like "political correctness," meant to replace traditional morality with a collective morality dictated by state policy. It is about expanding the reach of its control until it can dominate every element of each individual's life.

The enemy of socialism is not the political tyrant or Capitalism, because economic domination is what socialism's policies advocate. The enemy of socialism is the individual. Democratic Socialists believe and teach that citizens are incapable of true freedom without complete state intervention and that we need a new socialist vanguard to interpret and manage the relations between the state and the citizen. As early as the 1960s, socialist have taught the new slogan that "the personal is political."

Critical theory acts as a new lens through which people interpret the world. It encourages people to view all of history and all that exists in today's society through the Marxist worldview of class struggle. Every issue is one of the "oppressed" struggling against the "oppressor." This system of dialectical conflict is held by Marxist as the tool for socialism's evolution toward communism.

People who study critical theory will read a classic book but come to a radically different interpretation from that of someone who has not been indoctrinated by Marxist thought. Rather than read the story as it is, they will interpret it through the lens of an oppressed individual or an oppressed group struggling with an oppressor.

Stories become no longer about heroism, personal growth, or moral choice. Instead, everything becomes a story about the Marxist-Leninist worldview of struggle. And the conclusion it gives to resolve this struggle is to give absolute power to the state. The system of self-brainwashing under critical theory has become a cornerstone of modern education. It is the intentional planting of notions, altering of conclusions, and changing of the way people perceive information.

Critical theory is founded on the idea that all social dynamics are tyrannical and have been throughout history. Therefore, it must rewrite history, redefine all culture and social values, and replace them with a socialist state of absolute tyranny. This socialist tyranny, in its drive toward communism, has led to more than 100 million unnatural deaths over the last century. In its fight to end slavery and oppression of some, it enslaves and oppresses all of society.

The idea that "the personal is political," plays on the belief that in things like "identity politics," and holds that a person is no longer responsible for personal issues. At this point, things like personal behavior, responsibility and personal issues with others become the business of politics—of state control.

All human beings have natural rights – either endowed by their Creator or inherent in their nature, depending on whom you ask – and have a moral obligation to respect the rights of others. Natural rights impose the negative obligation not to interfere with someone else's liberty. Thus, it is morally unlawful to use coercion against someone who does not first undertake the use of force.

This kind of freedom involves far more than simple democracy. It demands a protected personal life within which an individual can pursue his freely chosen norms, actions, and ends without the arbitrary intervention of others. And this freedom is necessary for individual morality.

There can be no individual morality without personal responsibility and no personal responsibility without self-determination. Responsible self-determination implies rationality, honesty, self-control, productiveness, and perseverance. In order to provide the maximum self-determination for each individual, the state must be limited to maintaining justice and defending against internal or external coercion, thus protecting life, liberty, and property.

A socialist system can be moral in its effects if it promotes the possibility and likelihood of moral behavior by individuals who act within it. In this context, there is a moral imperative to create a political and economic system that permits the greatest possibility for self-determination and moral agency. Democratic Socialism is not that system.

No economic system can make people good or bad. But morality and virtue require that individuals be free to be immoral and of bad character. Only when an individual has choice and bears responsibility for his actions can he be moral.

Socialism theoretically permits individuals to spend less time focused on meeting physical needs, leaving them more time to engage in higher pursuits, by removing the individual of responsibility for personal behavior and its inevitable consequences through the denial and eventual suppression individual free will.

In 2020, Socialist Democrats seem to characterize fiscal responsibility something like this, "A $19 trillion national debt means that the federal government hasn't spent enough to solve our problems." Stealing money that belongs to others through taxation is perfectly alright if you spend it on good things. Apparently, people become much more honest, fair, competent, and compassionate once they get elected to office.

Some more of my favorite quotes from socialist politicians and recent candidates; "If you force employers to pay someone more than their services are worth; they will hire them anyway and just eat the difference." "Regulations always do good because their advocates mean well." "Civilizations rise and become great because they punish success and subsidize failure, then they collapse when they embrace freedom and free enterprise." "Each person is entitled to whatever he wants other people to pay for, like free college and birth control."

Proponents of the democratic socialist agenda will face resistance not only from American capitalists, but from basic math. Their promises, which include free college, a single-payer health care system, guaranteed jobs, a government paid basic income, and more, would require astonishingly high expenditures that would cause the federal deficit to skyrocket. As with most government funded programs, the costs, aka; taxpayer burden will likely never be published. Making big promises is one thing; paying for them is another.

Let's add up the cost of the popular far-left proposals. The Mercatus Center at George Mason University estimated that Sanders's Medicare-for-all plan would cost the government $32 trillion over the next decade, setting off an intense debate. But let's do the math using only figures from nonpartisan and even left-leaning groups.

To begin with the necessary context: The Congressional Budget Office assumes a baseline budget deficit of $12.4 trillion over the next decade, based on laws currently in effect. And even these projections assume that last year's tax cuts expire on schedule.

From this baseline, Sanders has proposed a Social Security expansion, including higher cost-of-living adjustments and higher minimum benefit levels, that the

Tax Policy Center estimates will cost $188 billion over the next decade.

The Tax Policy Center also values the Sanders and AOC "free college" proposal at $807 billion over the next decade. Next, the center estimates that Sanders's proposal of up to 12 weeks of paid family leave for new parents and for people with serious health conditions would cost another $270 billion.

Those costs, however, pale beside the cost of replacing private insurance, including copayments, with a Medicare-for-all plan. The Urban Institute estimates that Sanders's single-payer health plan would add $32 trillion in federal costs over the decade. Note that that's the exact same figure produced by those George Mason libertarians.

Alexandria Ocasio-Cortez and Senate Democrats also want to guarantee a job "for anyone who wants one," at $15 per hour plus benefits. The liberal Center on Budget and Policy Priorities commissioned a report by outside scholars Darrick Hamilton, William Darity, and Mark Paul that estimates the cost of a more modest proposal along these lines (with a lower wage, for example). It suggested the cost would be $56,000 apiece for 9.7 million enrollees, for a total of $6.8 trillion over the next decade. I expect the projected enrollment for the jobs program is a bit low.

The Center on Budget and Policy Priorities-commissioned report assumes nearly all participants would come from the ranks of the jobless who are seeking work. Realistically, the 60 million Americans currently earning less than $15 per hour (plus many retirees and longtime labor force dropouts) would also stampede into this program.

The report allows that employers would retain current workers with large raises, or a higher minimum wage. But clearly some of these 60 million workers would be laid off and possibly replaced with automation, particularly in industries with tight profit margins. Those job losses would expand this program's participation, as would an influx of workers who simply want an easier job or more hours than their current jobs.

Finally, Senate Democrats have promised $1 trillion for new infrastructure, and House Democrats are rallying around legislation to pay off all $1.4 trillion in student loan debt — both of which are on the Socialist agenda. Total cost: $42.5 trillion in new proposals over the next decade, on top of the $12.4 trillion baseline deficit.

To put this in perspective, Washington is currently projected to collect $44 trillion in revenues over the next decade. And the Republican tax cut, decried universally by Democrats as irresponsible, and considered to be financial "Armageddon" by House Speaker Nancy Pelosi will cost less than $2 trillion over the decade.

The 30-year projected tab for these programs is $218 trillion, on top of an $84 trillion baseline deficit driven by Social Security, Medicare, and the resulting interest costs. Federal spending, which typically ranges between 18 and 22 percent of GDP, would immediately soar past 40 percent of GDP on its way to nearly 50 percent within three decades thereby exceeding the current spending level of every country in Europe.

These numbers come from the Congressional Budget Office, top think tanks, and the lawmakers themselves. They are the left's own figures. Nevertheless, many advocates claim that single-payer health care will not worsen America's fiscal problem and may even be part of the solution. The math suggests otherwise. Let's see.

First, single-payer would not fix the current unsustainable health spending. Medicare's existing $6 trillion cash shortfall over the next decade, which soars to a $40 trillion shortfall over 30 years, would not be reduced because Medicare is already a price-controlled, single-payer system that would merely become more generous under Medicare-for-all.

Second, proponents claim that the $32 trillion single-payer cost should be considered differently from the other expenditures, since theoretically, money currently being spent by citizens on health insurance and other health-care costs would now be spent by the government. In other words, the money would be paid to the government as taxes and would then be redistributed and health care cost. What could possibly go wrong?

The Urban Institute math indicates otherwise. The $4 trillion saved by state and local governments on programs like Medicaid and CHIP over 10 years, and the $22 trillion saved by families and businesses on premiums and out-of-pocket expenses cannot easily be converted into a $26 trillion single-payer tax without serious economic and redistributive side effects.

The CBO data suggest that a new payroll tax, which is one of the "pay-fors" Sanders has emphasized, would need to be set at 29 percent in order to raise $26 trillion over the decade. And that is on top of the existing 15.3 percent payroll tax and all other federal and state taxes.

Hardest hit would be the 77 million Medicaid recipients who currently pay no health insurance premiums (just limited copays), and thus would not receive any "insurance premium windfall" to help pay for their steep new taxes.

Overall, converting these $26 trillion in savings into a "single-payer tax" is so difficult that Sanders's own page of tax increase options comes up with just $16 trillion. Those tax estimates are not independently verified, are often politically unrealistic, and fail to account for any revenues lost to interactions between tax proposals or macroeconomic responses.

What's more, even if Washington *could* tax all $26 trillion saved by families, businesses, and state governments, there remains a final $6 trillion federal cost that represents the increase in total national health spending.

Regardless of whether national health expenditures slightly rise or fall, virtually every analysis — liberal or conservative — agrees that Washington must come up with roughly $30 trillion to finance single-payer health care. And here is a key point: Even setting aside the feasibility of a 40 percent cut to health providers, I have yet to come across even one specific single-payer proposal that raises anywhere close to the roughly $30 trillion needed to pay for the new system.

Under the most generous assumptions possible, liberal proposals would cut $8.5 trillion on the spending side. To begin with, state governments no longer burdened with health care costs would save $4.1 trillion, according to the Urban Institute. The popular socialist goal of slashing defense spending down to Europe's target of 2 percent of GDP, would save $1.9 trillion according to CBO data.

Charitably assuming that the jobs guarantee would reduce antipoverty spending by one-quarter would save $2.5 trillion. Paying for the remaining $34 trillion would require nearly doubling federal tax revenues.

Where will the money come from to support all this democratic socialism? Using the CBO numbers, basic math, and Bernie Sanders' recommendations, the Fed would:

Tax corporations and rich families by seizing roughly 100 percent of all corporate profits as well as 100 percent of all family wage income and pass-through business income above the thresholds of $90,000 (single) or $150,000 (married), and absurdly assuming they all continue working, or.

Implement a value-added tax, which is basically a national sales tax. A rate of 87 percent would be needed to collect $34 trillion under the American tax base, or.

Create a new 37 percent payroll tax, on top of the existing 15.7 percent payroll tax, in order to collect $34 trillion.

And there is still the aforementioned baseline budget deficit of $12.4 trillion over the decade, and $84 trillion over 30 years. These are driven almost exclusively by growing Social Security and Medicare shortfalls as the Boomer population ages.

Since it is not sustainable to allow budget deficits to swell to nearly 10 percent of GDP during peace and prosperity, it would require an additional across-the-board income tax hike of 15 percentage points just to pay for the growing costs of our current federal programs. That means a probable federal income tax of around 67.7 percent.

Taxing the rich is not enough. America would need to match, or even surpass, Europe's enormous tax burden on the middle class. There is no evidence that American voters will accept this level of taxation.

Democratic socialists are purposely vague about the exorbitant tax burden they require. Alexandria Ocasio-Cortez recently offered a list of tax increases such as a 28 percent corporate tax rate, a "Buffett tax" on millionaires, and carbon tax that collectively add up to just $2 trillion over the decade, according to the CBO.

More broadly, advocates often downplay the cost of their proposals by introducing them one at a time, hiding the cumulative costs, and recycling the same tax increases across different proposals. The democratic socialists must move beyond slogans and figure out how to pay for these proposals using the laws of basic math. Common core be damned.

Chapter 9

Identity Politics and Victimhood

In the U.S., debates on issues of power, politics, and social justice are largely conducted in terms of identity-based perspectives. Blacks, disabled people, women, Hispanics, transgendered people, gays, and several other allegedly marginalized groups have adopted historical records and experiential knowledge of oppressed identities to further their claims in the political arena.

Identity politics began about five decades ago. It, too, had its founding fathers: militants who were influenced by the Marxist thinking then starting to sweep U.S. universities. They intimidated those administrators who did not already agree with them into forging the new group identities of which Herbert Marcuse taught, and divided Americans in the process.

The founders of La Raza, a group that essentially created the Hispanic identity, were steeped in militancy. Herman Gallegos learned community organizing from socialist Saul Alinsky. Ernesto Galarza, the "dean of Chicano activism," also went to establish La Raza Unida, and was instrumental in the work of Cesar Chavez, with whom he collaborated. Finally, Julian Samora, known as the father of Latino Studies, was educated at the culturally Marxist Frankfurt School.

Angela Davis, the Black Panther who teaches about multiculturalism today, said, "Herbert Marcuse taught me that it was possible to be an academic, an activist, a scholar, and a revolutionary." Yuji Ichioka, the radical Berkeley student who first coined the term "Asian-American," was another Marxist devotee. He founded the

Asian-American Political Alliance, an organization philosophically influenced by the works of Chairman Mao and the Black Panther movement.

These activists and administrators confected the groups we have today—such as Hispanics, Asians, Pacific Islanders, or the MENA designation Barack Obama had intended for Americans originating in the Middle East and North Africa. These struggles have shaped the development of both empirical and theoretical scholarship across disciplines such as social psychology, literature, and philosophy.

University of California San Diego Professor John Skrentny vividly depicts how top-down and undemocratic the genesis of identity politics was. The true iconic images of the era, he wrote, were "mostly not of angry minority protests, raised fists, picket lines, and placards. The images of the minority rights revolution are mostly of mainstream Euro-American males and minority advocates, wearing suits, sitting at desks, firing off memos, and meeting in government buildings to discuss new socialist policy directions."

And therein lies the problem. Power shoved down the people's throat is being rejected here and in Europe, especially on this issue of identity, in a collectivist context. By contrast, feminist legal scholarship in the U.S. has been slow to enter the identity-based battle. The significant victories accomplished by the women's movement have been won in the judicial and legislative arenas in the context of individual rights rather than depending on group identity.

A philosophical discussion of identity politics would focus on what binds people together for a common purpose. What convinces people to form their own nation? The philosopher Leo Strauss made a bona fide case that the Founding Fathers were in a state of nature, and then went on to forge the nation "to secure the blessings of liberty to ourselves and our posterity," in the words of the United States Constitution.

In contrast, identity politics offers an arrangement by different identity groups to engage in power-sharing and collaborate in the public sphere, while returning to their respective individual attachments at night. This is what has been historically defined as, "An association of racial, ethnic, and cultural subnational groups held together by the hopes for the material gains that can be provided by a planned economy and a compliant Socialist government."

John Stuart Mill stated, "Free institutions are next to impossible in a country made up of different nationalities," he said. "Among a people without fellow-feeling, especially if they read and speak different languages, the united public opinion, necessary to the working of representative government, cannot exist." Do we risk destroying a nation of individualistic freedom in the name of eradicating structural racism and "perceived unconscious bias," or do we reorder American society along communal, cultural and civic lines?

A debate without animosity might involve the question of immigration and the number of immigrants let in. Many Democratic Socialists do not understand that assimilation into a common national identity, into a "civil, free society" is harder when a society has a large number of foreign-born individuals. Assimilation into a dominant culture becomes much harder as the numbers of immigrants rise relative to the native population. As immigrant communities reach a certain scale, they tend to become self-sufficient and no longer need connections to groups outside themselves.

Sovereign nations can put their interests first without threatening democratic institutions and norms. Defenders of Socialism should acknowledge that controlling borders is a legitimate exercise of sovereignty, and that the appropriate number and type of immigrants is a legitimate subject for debate.

Denouncing citizens concerned about immigration as bigots improves neither the substance nor the politics of the problem. There's nothing anti-socialist about the perspective that too many immigrants stress a country's resources and capacity to absorb them, so that a reduction or even a pause may be in order. No issue has done more than immigration to feed populism and finding a sustainable compromise would drain much of the vitriol from today's politics.

We are at an unprecedented moment in America. For the first time in US history, white Americans are faced with the prospect of becoming a minority in the U.S. Many in our multicultural cities celebrate the ethnic diversity of America as a welcome step away from white supremacy. However, it is safe to say that large numbers of conservative whites are increasingly anxious about this phenomenon because of the open hostility toward whites encouraged and officially sanctioned by Socialist Democrats.

Meanwhile, the coming demographic shift has done little to allay minority concerns about discrimination. A recent survey found that 43% of black Americans do not believe America will ever make the changes necessary to give blacks equal rights. Most disconcertingly, black on other races hate crimes have increased 30% since the 2016 election.

Human nature has demonstrated that when groups feel mistreated and disrespected, they close ranks and become more narrow-minded, more defensive, more punitive, more us-versus-them in their collective thinking. In America today, every group feels this way to some extent. Whites and blacks, Latinos and Asians, men and women, Christians, Jews, and Muslims, straight people and gay people, liberals and conservatives – all feel their groups are being attacked, bullied, persecuted, discriminated against.

Of course, one group's claims to feeling threatened and oppressed are often met by another group's disdain because it discounts their own feelings of persecution. This is the manipulative nature of identity politics.

This trend, combined with perceived inequality, is why we now see identity politics on both sides of the political spectrum. And it leaves the United States in a perilous new situation: almost no one is standing up for an America without identity politics, for an American identity that transcends and unites all the country's many subgroups because it doesn't serve the Socialist narrative.

Dr Martin Luther King Jr proclaimed: "When the architects of our republic wrote the magnificent words of the Constitution and the Declaration of Independence, they were signing a promissory note to which every American was to fall heir. This note was a promise that *all men* would be guaranteed the unalienable rights of life, liberty, and the pursuit of happiness." Race was not a consideration because it is irrelevant. All lives matter.

Every human being has the same rights. Some prefer to make race an issue because it serves as a cultural crutch that justifies their victimhood. For others, it serves as a source of derision and self-proclaimed superiority. Neither holds true for everyone or even a majority of any race.

King's ideals for America that captured the imagination and hearts of the public and led to real change transcended group divides and called for an America in which skin color didn't matter. Leading liberal philosophical movements of that era were similarly group blind and universalist in character. At roughly the same time, the idea of universal human rights proliferated, advancing the dignity of every individual as the foundation of a just social order.

While all but a few ultra-conservatives have always been concerned with the oppression of minorities and the rights of disadvantaged groups, the dominant ideals in this period tended to be group blind, often cosmopolitan, with many calling for transcending not just ethnic, racial, and gender barriers.

In the 1980s and 1990s, a growing awareness that racial blindness was being used by conservatives to oppose policies intended to redress racial inequities, a new movement began to unfold on the left emphasizing group consciousness, group identity, and group discrimination claims.

Throughout history, many have noticed that the leading Socialist figures in America, whether in law, government, or academia, were predominantly white men and that the neutral "group-blind" invisible hand of the market wasn't doing much to correct long-standing imbalances.

With the collapse of the Soviet Union, the anti-capitalist economic preoccupations of the old Socialist Democrats began to take a backseat to a new way of understanding oppression. The Socialist politics of redistribution was replaced by a "politics of recognition". Modern identity politics was born.

Sonia Kruks writes, "What makes identity politics a significant departure from earlier movements is its demand for recognition on the basis of the very grounds on which recognition has previously been denied. Whether it is women, blacks, LGBTQs, pedophiles or any other collective, groups demand recognition. The demand is not for inclusion within the fold of 'universal humankind,' nor is it for respect 'in spite of one's differences.' Rather, what is demanded is respect for oneself as different."

In the U.S. today, blindness to group identity is the ultimate sin, because it masks the reality of group hierarchies and perceived oppression in America. It's just a fact that whites, and specifically white male Protestants, dominated America for most of its history, often violently, and that this legacy persists. The stubborn persistence of racial inequality in the wake of Barack Obama's supposedly "post-racial" presidency has left many young progressives disillusioned with the narratives of racial progress that were popular among liberals just a few years ago.

In recent years, the Democratic Socialist have upped the ante. A shift in tone, rhetoric, and logic has moved identity politics away from inclusion toward exclusion and division. As a result, many on the left have turned away from unifying and inclusive rhetoric, viewing it as an attempt to erase the specificity of the experience and oppression of historically marginalized minorities.

This deliberate exclusivity is partly epistemological, claiming that out-group members cannot share in the knowledge possessed by in-group members ("You can't understand X because you are white"; "You can't understand Y because you're not a woman"; "You can't speak about Z because you're not queer"). The idea of "cultural appropriation" insists, among other things, "These are our group's symbols, traditions, patrimony, and out-group members have no right to them."

According to the Democratic Socialist dogma, anyone who speaks in favor of unity or refuses to group others by race and ethnicity is labeled as indifferent to or even guilty of oppression. For some, especially on college campuses, anyone who doesn't swallow the socialists' anti-oppression orthodoxy without question and anyone who doesn't acknowledge "white supremacy" in America is a racist.

When Bernie Sanders told supporters, "It's not good enough for somebody to say, 'Hey, I'm a Latina, vote for me,' " Quentin James, a leader of Hillary Clinton's outreach efforts to people of color, retorted that Sanders's "comments regarding identity politics suggest he may be a white supremacist, too." Of course he is. If any of the self-proclaimed Democratic Socialists were genuinely concerned with equality, they would liquidate their mansions and other financial holdings and distribute the proceeds among the groups they claim to support.

Although inclusivity is presumably still the ultimate goal, the Democratic Left is pointedly exclusionary. During a Black Lives Matter protest at the DNC held in Philadelphia in July 2016, a protest leader announced that "this is a black and brown resistance march", asking white allies to "appropriately take their place in the back of this march." How is that not the exact kind of racism blacks experienced in Rosa Parks day? Because it is retaliatory does not make it "not-racism."

This brings us to the most striking feature of today's right-wing identity politics that has mobilized around the idea of whites as an endangered, discriminated-against group. In part this development carries forward a long tradition in America. But white identity politics has also gotten a tremendous recent boost from the Left, whose relentless berating, shaming, and bullying might have done more damage than good.

One white person at a political rally recently claimed that "I'm just so sick of being called a bigot that my anger at the authoritarian left has pushed me to support this anyone but a Democrat." "The Democratic party," said Bill Maher, "made the white working man feel like your problems aren't real because you're 'mansplaining' and check your privilege. You know, if your life sucks, your problems are real." When blacks blame today's whites for slavery or demand reparations, many white Americans feel as though they are being attacked for the sins of other generations.

The following blog post in the American Conservative has been share repeatedly and is worth quoting at length in this book because its relevance to this topic:

I'm a white guy. I'm a well-educated intellectual who enjoys small arthouse movies, coffeehouses and classic blues. If you didn't know any better, you'd probably mistake me for a lefty urban hipster.

And yet. I find some of the alt-right stuff exerts a pull even on me. Even though I'm smart and informed enough to see through it. It's seductive because I am not a person with any power or privilege, and yet I am constantly bombarded with messages telling me that I'm a cancer, I'm a problem, everything is my fault.

I am very lower middle class. I've never owned a new car and do my own home repairs as much as I can to save money. I cut my own grass, wash my own dishes, buy my clothes from Walmart. I have no clue how I will ever be able to retire. But oh, brother, to hear the media tell it, I am just drowning in unearned power and privilege, and America will be a much brighter, more loving, more peaceful nation when I finally just keel over and die.

Trust me: After all that, some of the alt-right stuff feels like a warm, soothing bath. A "safe space," if you will. I recoil from the uglier stuff, but some of it— the "hey, white guys are actually okay, you know! Be proud of yourself, white man!" stuff is really VERY seductive, and it is only with some intellectual effort that I can resist the pull ... If it's a struggle for someone like me to resist the pull, I imagine it's probably impossible for someone with less education or cultural exposure.

For decades, the Right has claimed to be a bastion of individualism, a place where those who rejected the divisive identity politics of the Left found a home. For this reason, conservatives typically paint the emergence of white identity as having been forced on them by the tactics of the Left. As one political commentator puts it, "feeling as though they are under perpetual attack for the color of their skin, many on the right have become defiant of their whiteness, allowing it into their individual politics in ways they have not for generations."

The problem is not difficult to understand. While black Americans, Asian Americans, Hispanic Americans, Jewish Americans, and many others are allowed and encouraged to feel solidarity and take pride in their racial or ethnic identity, white Americans have for the last several decades been told they must never, ever do so.

People want to see their own group as exceptional, as something to be deeply proud of; that's what identity politics is all about. For decades now, non-whites in the United States have been encouraged to indulge their tribal instincts in just this way, but American whites have not. In 21st Century America, being born white is becoming a punishable offense, if not a crime, and is something one should be ashamed of.

Chapter 10

Cultural Differences

Culture is inherently collective in nature. Cultural differences are the various beliefs, behaviors, languages, practices and expressions considered unique to members of a specific ethnic group, race or national origin. Differences between people within any given nation or culture are much greater than differences between ethnic groups. Education, social standing, religion, personality, belief structure, past experience, affection shown in the home, and a myriad of other factors affects human behavior and group culture.

Race has become a dominant social reality and an important and enduring component of group identity. However, culture is much deeper and more inclusive than race alone. While race is often distinguished on the basis of physical characteristics, especially skin color, ethnic distinctions generally focus on such cultural characteristics as language, history, religion, and customs.

Ethnicity is similar in concept to race. However, what begins as an ethnic or cultural distinction often becomes racialized, and racial groups are often identified, in the public mind, with reference to customs and behavior. In this chapter we will look at racial and ethnic groups, without making any sharp distinction between these terms.

Historically, the recognition of new racial and ethnic groups in the U.S. population has often been marked by conflict, prejudice, and disparate treatment of racial and ethnic minorities. An early and enduring racial and ethnic distinction developed between the Native American Indian inhabitants of the continent and the European colonists.

The forcible importation into the American colonies of Africans as slaves gave rise to a third enduring racial or ethnic category. The definition of this category in the U.S. has varied over time, as it does in other countries, such as Brazil and South Africa. The United States held for several centuries to a rule that any African or African American ancestry defined a person as black.

Other waves of immigration have created and continue to create separately identified racial and ethnic groups in the United States. At the height of this immigration, European ethnic groups were often treated as distinct races in the census and other government statistics and heavily discriminated against. The Irish were racialized first by the British and later in American society.

Racial and ethnic distinctions among Americans of European origin are now generally subdued, and individuals manifest considerable variation in how much they identify with their European ancestry. This muting of distinctions is also observed in other racial and ethnic groups. Culturally, in the U.S., black Americans have resisted integration into other groups.

Hispanic and Asian immigration began early, some Hispanic settlements in fact predate the accession of particular territories to the United States. Immigration has greatly accelerated in recent decades, rising to levels that rival those of the earlier massive European immigrations. As in other waves of immigration, many Hispanics and early Asian immigrants have at least initially borne the burden of low-wage work and social inferiority even though often earning more than they would in their countries of origin.

Immigrant groups have immediately become part of the system of social stratification in U.S. society, generally starting at the bottom of the social ladder. While ethnic stratification has often given rise to racist ideologies that ascribe inherent inferiority to particular groups, individual access to valued resources such as jobs, income and wealth, education, economic and political prestige is generally earned over decades, for members of any ethnicity, willing to work for them.

In the U.S., this is still a plausible ideal. However, the social divisions required for Democratic Socialism to succeed have openly exacerbated the cultural differences in our American society. A common refrain from ethnic groups who perceive themselves as oppressed is that minority neighborhoods, schools, and property are valued lower than white or more affluent neighborhoods, schools, and property, *solely based on the races of the community members.*

Apparently, more whites than minorities attend and complete college degrees *solely because of white oppression of minorities.* More recently, although ninety percent of television show casts since 2009 are multi-racial, multi-gender, have at least one LGBTQ element, or exclusively Black casted; many of the involved actors and fans alike feel oppressed *because most of the script writers are white.* Not only are the writers and staff mostly white, it is somehow their fault that there are fewer black or minority writers!

The most prominent and historically explainable illustration for a discussion of cultural differences is probably the disparity between predominantly white and predominately minority communities. Certainly, there exceptions to every comparison. These exceptions are understood, appreciated, and congratulated by everyone, except those who view the success of some in their social group as betrayal of their race.

One example of this social misperception and fundamental attribution error is the idea that "If we can detect how much racism depletes wealth from black homeowners, we can begin to address bigotry, principally by giving black homeowners and policymakers a target price for redress. Laws have changed, but the value of assets like buildings, schools, leadership, and land itself are inextricably linked to the perceptions of black people."

I respectfully disagree. It is a property value and development fact that the value of assets like buildings, schools, and land itself are inextricably linked to the physical condition, social desirability, and potential restoration or development costs.

Statistically, in many major metropolitan areas across the U.S., homes in neighborhoods where the population is 50 percent or more black are valued at roughly half the price as homes in neighborhoods with no black residents. Homes of similar quality in neighborhoods with similar amenities are worth 23 percent less in majority black neighborhoods, compared to those with very few or no black residents.

It is often reported that neighborhoods with higher minority populations are more devalued, more segregated, have higher crime rates, and produce less upward mobility for the children who grow up in those communities as compared to predominantly white neighborhoods. What is seldom if ever addressed is how exactly does the valuation of homes and schools affect the upward mobility of children.

Children of all races and ethnicities have overcome greater obstacles than the local appraisal district's valuation of properties in their neighborhood to become successful, contributing members of society. Any disparity of upward mobility is bound by the cultural norms and perceptions of the social groups these children are raised with.

While property anywhere crime rates are elevated will be devalued, rental properties are generally the most negatively impacted. While this may be advantageous to renters, in so far as it results in a lower rental payment, the inevitable devaluation of owner-occupied housing in nearby neighborhoods makes it difficult for property owners to refinance, borrow, or sell at a perhaps higher valuation for the same property in a better maintained community.

It has been said that "structural characteristics of homes and neighborhood amenities do not fully explain the absolute difference in home value." While I would agree with that assessment, property upkeep and community maintenance are certainly major contributing factors property values. Pride in one's personal property, a family home, and community is a cultural trait and is generally taught by an older generation to a younger generation.

Most protagonists of racial bias say things like, "If properties in black neighborhoods were priced like those in white neighborhoods, black children would have more wealth to draw upon to pay for things like private schooling, tutoring, travel, and higher education."

Historically, disparities have existed in access to homeownership by low-income and minority households. The factors that shape, impede, or facilitate homeownership opportunities for these households have been the subject of substantial research, including studies commissioned by HUD's Office of Policy Development and Research in the early to mid-2000s.

One focus of these inquiries, arising from concerns about fairness and discrimination, has been differences in homeownership rates across income and racial or ethnic groups. The persistence of these disparities, according to a body of related research, suggests that demographic and economic factors play a significant role in shaping homeownership trends.

Analyses of the composition of the homeownership gap have concluded that socioeconomic variables explain approximately 80 percent of the difference, leaving roughly

20 percent of the disparity attributable to discrimination and unidentified influences.

Homeownership decisions are also shaped by patterns of household formation that differ by economic, demographic, and social circumstances. Cultural factors that affect household formation include racial and ethnic differences, age structure of the population, marriage and divorce patterns, and typical leaving-home ages.

Nonetheless, if one's socio-cultural group limits independent thinking and promotes victim hood and a welfare class identity, it is easy to blame one's economic status on discrimination.

The relative importance of family culture and good role models varies among blacks and whites. While whites attribute family culture and good role models as major reasons for their self-perception. Forty-three percent of blacks say a lack of motivation to work hard may be holding blacks back. Still, many blacks say these items are no more important than lower quality schools, discrimination, and lack of jobs. Cultural differences in perspective maybe?

Is race and ethnicity an issue in the U.S.? Absolutely. However, given the plethora of minority focused social and economic assistance available specifically to non-whites, one has to wonder why. Literally thousands of minorities avail themselves of these programs and overcome poverty, joblessness, and other obstacles to social upward mobility.

For some, social oppression serves to justify their apathetic complacency. Decades of growth in the welfare state have incentivized ethnic minorities to avoid personal responsibility for supporting their families, learning marketable skills, and becoming productive members of American society.

For others, the propagation of racial oppression is a vehicle used to manipulate discrimination of social groups for political and personal gain, all the while feigning support for the oppressed. The remainder of this chapter is an illustration of the differences in political culture between a Republican or Capitalist mindset and a Democrat or Socialist mindset in the context of government funded programs for racial equality.

Numerous peer reviewed studies have been published over the past 60 years on the topic of race or ethnicity based national policies and the effect of bipartisan politics. Although the topic of racial equality is no less important on one side of the political arena than the other, there is far more prejudice among Democratic Socialists than there is among Republican Capitalists.

The reason for this differential impact is not difficult to understand once the different political perspectives of capitalists and socialists are considered. Whether capitalists are prejudiced or not, they are united by a commitment to the principle of limited government, at least when it comes to the social welfare and economic role of the national government.

As a consequence, and precisely because they support free enterprise and equal opportunity for all, capitalists see no compelling reason why ethnic minorities should receive any special treatment or even significant welfare assistance from the government.

Traditionally, capitalists oppose a major role for the national government in providing for the general welfare, and thereby having control, of the citizenry. This opposition to government involvement applies to the lives of minorities just as it does to whites. Thus, in following long-accepted and practiced Republican ideology, capitalists generally oppose government aid to minorities.

The situation is quite different among Socialists. Given their general support for an activist government and the increased contribution that blacks have made to the Democratic electoral coalition in recent presidential elections, their natural inclination is to support substantial government aid for various groups, especially African-Americans.

However, fiscally conservative Democrats do not share this outlook. Instead, they take exactly the opposite position of opposing government assistance and special treatment for minorities. In other words, Socialism is difficult for conservative Democrats to embrace because they are less inclined to support government programs to assist minorities but are committed to Green New Deal government activism.

Prejudice against minorities plays a major role in shaping the political thinking of Socialists, a minor one in shaping the thinking of Capitalists. Statistical correlations between welfare policy positions and minority prejudice among white Republicans are for all intents and purposes negligible.

Statistical evidence clearly indicates that prejudice plays little or no role in shaping the racial policy preferences of Capitalists. Not surprisingly, the correlations for Independents tend to fall between those for Socialists and Capitalists, but it is the striking differences between the latter two groups that is impressive.

The statistics regarding the probabilities of strong Democrats reveal a marked steepness; their degree of support for racial equality welfare policies is strongly affected by personal as well as group prejudice. In other words, the statistics show that racial prejudice has a much greater influence on minority welfare policy preferences of Democrats than on those of Republicans.

In the U.S. recent election results indicate a large portion of the American electorate is becoming increasingly disenchanted with government supported activism, and this is particularly true among key groups such as blue-collar workers and conservatives. Many Democrats may have become disillusioned with their party's commitment to Socialist programs. Frankly, I believe this disenchantment is less a function of attitudes toward minorities and more a function of opposition to government activism.

In other words, Democrats who dislike minorities may be Socialists in name only, opposed not only to policies designed to help minorities but to the whole philosophy of social welfare favored by the Democratic party at least since the New Deal.

Socialists who embrace minorities believe that government should increase spending to reduce unemployment, to favor narrowing the gap between rich and poor, and get angry over special benefits like tax breaks going to the richest people and biggest businesses and the lack of affordable medical care for people who do not have jobs.

A notable difference along the lines of racial equality for Democratic policy-makers regarding Black Americans is the prejudice among white Democrats. In other words, it is racial attitudes, not social welfare policies, that drive a wedge through the Democratic Socialist movement. Racial prejudice remains a politically powerful force in the Democratic Party.

The Republican party appears to be the new home of racial equality policy. Republicans, particularly Capitalists, whatever their level of prejudice, are committed to a limited role for the national government in the social welfare domain.

Presumably, the reason why minority tolerant Republicans do not translate these sentiments into support for government activism is because they believe that the national government is an inappropriate vehicle for this purpose. For, at the same time, they are significantly more likely to support private initiatives in civil rights than their more minority prejudiced co-partisans.

Chapter 11

Democratic Socialism – Somewhere Between Democracy and Tyranny

According to data compiled by Freedom House (2020), democracy has been in a recession for over a decade, and more countries have lost rather than gained civil and political rights each year.

In the Philippines, President Rodrigo Duterte has seized even greater power and threatened martial law-style enforcement of a monthlong lockdown. And in March 2020, the Hungarian Parliament passed the Coronavirus Act, which grants Viktor Orbán's government unprecedented emergency powers for an indefinite period of time.

Still, research suggests that even though autocracies have introduced more stringent lockdowns, democracies have been more effective in reducing travel and the movement of people in their countries. Thus, while autocrats often seek to capitalize on perceived threats, their handling of the pandemic on these dimensions seems unlikely to look appealing to those accustomed to self-government.

In the West, American's have lived within the ideology of an elected and representative government. The truth, I have suspected for three decades, is quite different. This misperception was revealed when Barrack Obama was allegedly re-elected in 2012 and the private handlers and financiers of the Democratic Socialists and Muslim movement were uncovered. Enter the Deep State.

Prior to World War II, the United States government relied on the military intelligence apparatus and corporate espionage for surveillance matters. The aristocracy who ruled the federal government tended to view such activity as immoral and quasi-criminal.

This egotistical apprehension put the United States at a disadvantage compared with Great Britain, Germany, and Russia, all of which had sophisticated intelligence bureaus and happily spied on adversaries and allies alike.

In the US, "*deep state*" describes a hidden government within the elected government and many theorists believe that this shadow government comprises partly elected officials, partly industry leaders, and largely public service employees, united under a secret agenda.

The existence of the Deep State is not a recent discovery. While the apparatus itself has been around for over a century, the no-longer covert subterfuge by various political operatives has recently given it a name.

Memorable examples include President Kennedy's preference for using "back channels" for sensitive issues. This propensity quite probably help the U.S. avoid a war with Russia over the Bay of Pigs fiasco in early 1963. Simultaneously, Vice-President Lyndon Johnson was collaborating with the Deep State to undermine Kennedy's troop withdrawal from Vietnam at the time of the president's assassination.

Since at least the 1950s, main stream media have been used by national governments to gather information and influence public opinion. In 2007, a large cache of documents from the 1970s were declassified and released by the CIA. These documents, referred to as "The Family Jewels," documented the investigations into the CIA's misconduct of the media during the 1970s. Though declassified documents show that this type of operation occurred, it's never been officially acknowledged.

A memo from a staff person at the National Security Council was published in August 2017 in Foreign Policy. The memo suggests that U.S. President Donald Trump is being continuously attacked because he represents an "existential threat to the cultural Marxist memes that dominate the prevailing cultural narrative."

In 2019, Jason Chaffetz, former Chairman of the U.S. House Oversight Committee, describes the deep state as "a bureaucracy that allowed agencies to become weaponized in the service of political battles." He goes on to say that in the beginning "that meant protecting President Obama by using federal power to target political opponents or by covering the tracks of the corrupt or incompetent within his administration. By the time I left Congress, the deep state's focus had shifted to thwarting the administration of the newly elected President Donald Trump."

Okay, so what does a healthy society look like? A healthy society proactively avoids concentrating all power and resources in one party or person. This is more than just having multiple political parties and elections.

It is the deliberate structure of society so that layers of local government, private companies, private or local educational institutions, civic organizations, judicial and police systems, individuals with personal wealth, non-profits, and religious organizations act as a brake on any party or person that goes off the rails and attempts to implement a dictatorship over society as a whole.

A healthy society has private businesses that have to serve customers to stay in business. In a healthy society, politicians are given power by the people relating only to their function: legislating, performing legal judgments, or managing a specific, well-defined part of the government. Checks and balances with other offices of government are implemented to further reduce the concentration of power for government officials.

As of the date of publication of this book, a pandemic sweeps the globe, it is carrying with it a related and equally dangerous threat to free speech and open discourse. The firing of military commanders for the political crime of raising the alarm over the spreading viral risk to military troops living in close quarters.

Another example is the practice or ruining a scientist's career and incarcerating them without an arraignment for questioning the efficacy of vaccination derived from animal tissue is among the most vivid examples of a metastasizing trend of silencing and punishing speech, presumably to protect public health and order.

Emergencies have always been used as justifications to curb free speech in the name of keeping secrets, suppressing disloyalty, and aiding the war effort. While extreme measures may now seem warranted and urgent to help halt the contagion, a series of current trends pose serious risks for open expression, foreshadowing threats that are likely to endure long after the lockdown has lifted.

Many of these measures have less to do with public health than they do with protecting political and institutional reputations, and with trying to retake control of the devastating narrative of a pandemic that has fed on human failures of anticipation, preparation, and mobilization.

Unfortunately, while many of these Socialist trends tend to arise in authoritarian countries, others are taking root in democracies around the globe. The suppression of free speech impedes a population's effort to hold accountable the officials who are responsible for managing their nation.

The Philippines has threatened imprisonment for journalists who report what the government deems to be "false information." Thailand has authorized prison terms of up to five years for reporting what the government deems "is untrue" and may cause public dissention.

Voices that have traditionally spoken out against efforts to inform the public of critical information—such as the U.S. government and the European Union—have been mostly silent, mired in crafting their own politically advantageous crisis responses and guilty of their own ignorance.

With companies now collaborating with governments to collect, analyze, and operationalize masses of data on individuals' movements, temperatures, and contacts, the already limited protections for our online privacy are likely to be eliminated. Ambitious, app-based efforts to scale contact-tracing in the context of the pandemic could readily be repurposed by governments to track individuals' contacts with dissidents, political allies, and journalists.

Knowledge that the government has a way to track these types of associations would seem to infringe on freedom of speech and association as well as suppress political organizing efforts. The technologies powering these apps could inform governments to where we've been, whom we have seen, and what we have been talking about.

The powerful demonstration in the summer of 2020 regarding online platforms' ability to curb the flow of misinformation will likely inspire governments to demand that similarly aggressive measures be applied communications that the broadcast media, or an offended individual tags as anti-anything on a social media platform, relating to dissident groups that a government deems subversive.

The current conduct of governments could have lasting ramifications. As the immediate crisis subsides and attention turns to restarting the economy, there is no guarantee that public or political pressure will be powerful enough to ensure that pandemic-driven crackdowns on civil liberties don't outlast the contagion. Moreover, there is a risk that aspects of the battle against COVID-19 become a new "forever war," with privacy violations and censorship becoming semi-permanent on the justification that the virus, and its inevitable successors, can never be fully vanquished.

Robert Newell's article for the *Foundation for Economic Education* provides an excellent summary in closing so I have included the opening paragraphs here. On the surface, democracy seems to encompass all social ideals and appears to be the epitome of political government. The motivating principle asserts the inherent right of all to participate in government and determine public policy. But with unquestioned power invested in popular opinion, democratic idealism deteriorates rapidly into government by organized majorities.

Even the authoritarian majorities who imagine themselves self-governed have no real understanding of political subterfuge and simply endorse whatever their leaders are pleased to tell them. And since it is easier to subjugate and manipulate those who believe themselves free, the grand illusion of freedom and self-government is carefully preserved by the strategists who constantly maneuver behind the democratic stage.

Since democracy is not of itself a stable form of government, but rather a method of ordaining social change, all forms of political tyranny can easily win the endorsement of the majority. The irresponsible elements of any society are readily persuaded to state-sponsored beggary on the assurance their personal problems will be miraculously solved by some political nostrum a clever candidate advises them to try. To exercise control over an apparently self-governed democracy is only to understand and utilize the principles of Social Conditioning. The demagogues who successfully exploit social and economic disorders and identify themselves with the majority, ultimately attaining just another oligarchy.

References

Abbey, Ruth and Fredrick Appel. 1999. Domesticating Nietzsche: A Response to Mark Warren," Political Theory, 27: 121.

Coles, Romand. 1996. "Liberty, Equality, and Receptive Generosity: Neo-Nietzschean Reflections on Ethics and Politics of Coalition," American Political Science Review 90:375.

Collins, James. 1972. Interpreting Modern Philosophy. Princeton: Princeton University Press.

Connolly, William. 1991. Identity/Difference. Ithaca: Cornell University Press.

Freud, Sigmund. 1961. Civilization and Its Discontents. New York: W.W. Norton.

Frey, C B, G Presidente, C Chen (2020), "Democracy, Culture, and Contagion: Political Regimes and Countries Responsiveness to Covid-19", Covid Economics 18.

Hatab, Lawrence. 1995. A Nietzschean Defense of Democracy, Chicago: Open Court.

Honig, Bonnie. 1993. Political Theory and the Displacement of Politics. Ithaca: Cornell University Press.

Mussolini, Benito. 2001. "The Doctrine of Fascism." Ideals and Ideologies: A Reader.

Terence Ball and Richard Dagger, eds. New York: Longman.

Nietzsche, Friedrich. 1968. Will to Power. New York: Vintage Books.

Nietzsche, Friedrich. 2003. Beyond Good and Evil. New York: Penguin Classics, 2003.

Nietzsche, Friedrich. 1999. On the Genealogy of Morals. New York: Oxford University Press.

Nietzsche, Friedrich. 2000. The Antichrist. Amherst: Prometheus Books.

Nietzsche, Friedrich. 1974. The Gay Science. New York: Vintage Books.

Nietzsche, Friedrich. 1992. Ecce Homo. New York: Penguin Classics.

Nietzsche, Friedrich. 1998. Twilight of the Idols, New York: Oxford University Press.

Oakeshott, Michael. 1962. "On Being Conservative." Reprinted in Ideals and Ideologies.

Owen, Robert. 2001. "Address to the Inhabitants of New Lanark." Ideals and Ideologies: A Reader. Terence Ball and Richard Dagger, eds. New York: Longman.

Plato. 1991. The Republic. Allan Bloom, ed. New York: Basic Books.

Rousseau, Jean Jacques. 1988. *The Social Contract*. G.D.H. Cole, ed. New York: Prometheus Books.

Russell, H. (1944). Tyranny and Democracy. The Classical Weekly, 37(11), 128-130. doi:10.2307/4341855

Warren, Mark. 1985. "Nietzsche and Political Philosophy," Political Theory, 13: 183.

Warren, Mark. 1998. "Political Readings of Nietzsche,"
Political Theory, 16: 90.

Woolfolk, Alan. 1986. "On Warren's 'Nietzsche and Political
Philosophy,'" Political Theory, 14: 51.

Fred Magdoff and Michael D. Yates (November
2009). "What Needs To Be Done: A Socialist
View". Monthly Review. Retrieved 2014-02-23.

Let's produce for use, not profit. Retrieved August 7, 2010,
from worldsocialism.org: "Archived copy". Archived
from the original on July 16, 2010. Retrieved August
18, 2015.

Professor Richard D. Wolff (2009-06-29). "Economic Crisis
from a Socialist Perspective". Rdwolff.com. Archived
from the original on 2014-02-28. Retrieved 2014-02-23.

Engels, Fredrich. Socialism: Utopian and Scientific.
Retrieved October 30, 2010, from
Marxists.org: http://www.marxists.org/archive/marx/work
s/1880/soc-utop/ch03.htm, "The bourgeoisie demonstrated
to be a superfluous class. All its social functions are now
performed by salaried employees."

The Political Economy of Socialism, by Horvat, Branko.
1982. Chapter 1: Capitalism, The General Pattern of
Capitalist Development (pp. 15–20)

Marx and Engels Selected Works, Lawrence and Wishart,
1968, p. 40. Capitalist property relations put a "fetter" on
the productive forces.

Rogers, Heather. "The Conquest of Garbage" isreview.org.
International Socialist Review (1997). Retrieved 2008-03-
13.

Hawken, Paul. "Natural Capitalism". Retrieved 2008-03-13.

U.S. EPA. "Municipal Solid Waste (MSW) Pie Chart". Retrieved 2008-03-13.

Inman, Phillip (2006-09-30). "When your iPod isn't all that it's cracked up to be". London: The Guardian. Retrieved 2008-03-13.

McMinn, David. "Planned Obsolescence: The Ultimate Economic Inefficiency". Retrieved 2008-03-13.

PBS Frontline (9 November 2004). "Interview with Naomi Klein". Retrieved 2008-03-13.

Brander, James A. Government policy toward business. 4th ed. Mississauga, Ontario: John Wiley & Sons Canada, Ltd., 2006. Print.

Vladimir Lenin. "Imperialism: The Highest Stage of Capitalism". Retrieved 2008-02-26.

"Socialism and Man in Cuba" A letter to Carlos Quijano, editor of Marcha, a weekly newspaper published in Montevideo, Uruguay; published as "From Algiers, for Marcha: The Cuban Revolution Today" by on March 12, 1965

"Best Sellers From 1987's Book Crop". The New York Times. Retrieved 13 October 2011.

Ravi Batra (1990). Regular economic cycles: money, inflation, regulation and depressions, Venus Books, 1985. Investment Library. ISBN 9781863500289. Retrieved 13 October 2011.

"Working Paper No. 589" (PDF). Levyinstitute.org. Retrieved 2014-02-23.

"The Inheritance of Inequality" (PDF). Retrieved 2014-02-23.

Ravi Batra. "The Occupy Wall Street Movement and the Coming Demise of Crony Capitalism", Foreign Affairs, October 11, 2011". Archived from the original on 13 October 2011. Retrieved 13 October 2011.

Engels, Frederick. "On the Question of Free Trade". Retrieved 2008-03-11.

Easterling, Earl. "Marx's Theory of Economic Crisis". International Socialist Review. Retrieved 2008-03-13.

Marx, Karl. "The Communist Manifesto". Retrieved 2008-03-11.

Engels, Frederick. "Part III: Socialism (Theoretical) – Anti-Duhring". Retrieved 2008-03-11.

Proudhon, Pierre-Joseph. "What Is Property? An Inquiry Into the Principle of Right and Government". Retrieved 2008-03-10.

D'Amato, Paul (2006). The Meaning of Marxism. Haymarket Books. p. 60. ISBN 978-1931859295.

Anarchist Essays, pp. 22–23, 40. Freedom Press, London, 2000.

Carson, Kevin (2007). Studies in Mutualist Political Economy. BookSurge Publishing. ISBN 978-1419658693.

Landes, William M.; Posner, Richard A. "An Economic Analysis of Property Law". Retrieved 2008-03-10.

"Geregistreerd via Argeweb". Unpop.nl. Archived from the original on 2007-09-28. Retrieved 2014-01-11.

"Industrial metabolism: Restructuring for sustainable development". unu.edu. Retrieved 2014-01-11.

Jeroen C.J.M. van den Bergh and Harmen Verbruggen (1998-09-28). "EconPapers: Spatial Sustainability,

"Planning and Markets: Peter Gordon and Harry W. Richardson". -pam.usc.edu. Archived from the original on 2010-06-27. Retrieved 2014-01-11.

"Capitalism's Environmental Crisis – Is Technology the Answer?". monthlyreview.org. December 2000. Retrieved 2014-01-11.

Ahmed, Nafeez (August 27, 2018). "Scientists Warn the UN of Capitalism's Imminent Demise". Vice. Retrieved August 30, 2018.

Paddison, Laura (August 31, 2018). "We Cannot Fight Climate Change with Capitalism, Says Report". The Huffington Post. Retrieved September 2, 2018.

Bipartisan Millennial Housing Commission. 2002. "Meeting Our Nation's Housing Challenges." Washington, DC.

U.S. Department of Housing and Urban Development. 2010. "Barriers to Minority Homeownership."

Interview with Janneke Ratcliffe, September 2012.